A CELEBRATION OF WEAVERS

Catalog of Weavers and Baskets
of the Doris Borhauer Basket Collection
Sitka, Alaska

A project by the Sitka Tribe of Alaska
through a Historic Preservation Grant
from the
National Park Service

By
Helen Dianne Dangel, Cultural Research Specialist

THE
DONNING COMPANY
PUBLISHERS

This material is based upon work assisted by a grant from the Department of the Interior, National Park Service. Any opinions, findings, and conclusions or recommendations expressed in this material are those of the author(s) and do not necessarily reflect the views of the Department of the Interior.

First edition of this book was published in 2005 by the Sitka Tribe of Alaska.
This revised second edition is published in 2006 by the Donning Company Publishers.

The Donning Company Publishers
184 Business Park Drive, Suite 206
Virginia Beach, VA 23462

Steve Mull, General Manager
Barbara B. Buchanan, Office Manager
Richard A. Horwege, Senior Editor
Bobbi LaChance, Graphic Designer
Amy Thomann, Imaging Artist
Project Research Coordinator, Debby Dowell
Scott Rule, Director of Marketing
Stephanie Linneman, Project Director
Barbara Bolton, Project Director

Library of Congress Cataloging-In-Publication Data
A celebration of weavers : catalog of weavers and baskets of the Doris Borhauer Basket
Collection, Sitka, Alaska ; a project by the Sitka tribe of Alaska through a historic preserva-
tion grant from the National Park Service / compiled by Helen Dianne Dangel. — Rev. 2nd ed.
     p.   cm.
   "First edition of this book was published in 2005 by the Sitka Tribe of Alaska."
   Includes index.
   ISBN-13: 978-1-57864-358-5 (soft cover : alk. paper)
   ISBN-10: 1-57864-358-9 (soft cover : alk. paper)
1. Tlingit Indians. 2. Tlingit baskets. 3. Indians of North America—Alaska—
Sitka. 4. Sitka (Alaska)—Social life and customs. I. Dangel, Helen Dianne.
   E99.T6C45 2006
   746.41'2089972700747982—dc22
                      2006009114
Printed in the United States of America at Walsworth Publishing Company

TABLE OF CONTENTS

 Foreword

You are in for a treat. This book is easy to read and captures the stuff of life in Sitka on the outer coast of Alaska. If you are a person from the coast, you will recognize faces and names as you enjoy the baskets. For the collector or museum folks, you may recognize baskets by their designs, shape, and style then be able to put a face and name with the baskets you have known for years.

In the spring of 2005, an event honoring weavers called "A Celebration of Weavers" took place in Sitka, Alaska. In the spirit of this collection, descendants came in from neighboring villages to join the two surviving weavers for a community celebration. Many more stories of harvesting, ingenuity, and indigenous science were told. . . .

This catalog articulates the life that goes into these beautiful baskets through the weavers' stories. Without embellishing or interpreting the stories for the reader, this book allows us to have a first-person experience. For years, baskets have been presented as functional and anonymous. In this book, you will enjoy the textures and emotions as the weavers draw you into their world, stories of family ties, joys, and difficulties. It was basketry that helped the Tlingit transition from a subsistence lifestyle to a modern market economy.

Several of these baskets are very old; most of them come from the early 1900s up to 1967. I know how important this book is as a full-time basket weaver. It illustrates the connection to the natural elements, which the baskets still hold today. In our busy lives at the beginning of another century, the connection is fragile, but sustainable, and is a respectful relationship with place. This book recognizes the connections and will become a great tool to carry the stories of the past, as well as today's stories, forward. Grandmothers and aunties are continuing to share the skills and joy of weaving to the next generations. "From time immemorial," as my grandmother Eliza Jane Mork would say.

I encourage other communities to look at a project like this of your own. It speaks to the resilience of culture in today's world.

Gunalchéesh ho ho (Thank you), Helen.

Teri Rofkar
Sitka, Alaska

Acknowledgments

I would like to thank everyone who contributed to this project. Any mistakes are entirely my own, and not theirs. Those who were interviewed about the weavers deserve credit for their information, and without them, this project could not have happened. Those who were interviewed are Camille Ferguson, Robert Sam, Herman Kitka, Jean Boone-Hamar, Emily Williams, Delores Churchill, Irene Jimmy, Andréa Craig, Maria Guthrie, Agnes Bellinger, Della Cheney, Anne Johnson, Barbara Lewis, Donald Didrickson, Ida Peters, Mona Jackson, LaVerne Peters, Nelson Frank, Bertha Karras, Selina Everson, Steve Johnson Sr., Lucy Clewis, Helen Skeek, Mary Swanson, Selina Claggett, and Earl Williams Sr. Others who were consulted for this project include Anne Farquhar, Katie Davis, Erna Fawcett, Vesta Dominicks, Charles "Topsy" Johnson, Cherilyn Holter, and any others I might have forgotten to mention. Thank you to Harold Jacobs in particular for providing much information on Tlingit names, clans, and parents of weavers. Thank you to Bob Sam and Steve Johnson Jr. for providing answers to endless little questions. Thank you to my supervisor, Jessica Perkins, for providing advice, and doing last minute transcribing. Kathy Hope Erickson helped with the initial part of this project, thank you Kathy. A special thank you to Sue Thorsen, Ramona East, and Michele Simmons at Sitka National Historical Park. Sue provided her knowledge on old residents of Sitka and of the Basket Collection, Ramona for all her help photographing baskets, and Michele for helping set-up the Public Celebration. Thank you to Teri Rofkar for artistic advice, comments on basket design, and setting up the display of baskets. Thank you to Gail Peterson for providing space at Southeast Alaska Indian Cultural Center for the basket exhibit. Thank you to Peter Corey for supporting this project. Thank you to Shelley Stallings for teaching a workshop in Ketchikan at the "Gathering of Alaskan Basket Makers" on how to photograph baskets. Thank you, especially, to the Elders who came up with the idea for this project, and thank you to Robi Craig for writing the grant that got us here.

◪ Background

This catalog celebrates the weavers of the Doris Borhauer Basket Collection through a look at the weavers' lives and their weaving. This basket collection is unique in that it has notes for all of the baskets which provide details about the baskets and their weavers, such as the price of a particular basket and geneological information about the weavers. Steve Henrikson, curator for the Alaska State Museum, noted, "Most importantly is that the names of the weavers are recorded. In that regard this collection is undoubtedly the best for the time period it covers."

An Elder looks at a basket from the Doris Borhauer Basket Collection at a viewing during the Haa Kayaaní conference in May 2001.

The basket collection has ninety-two baskets woven by Tlingit and Haida women from Southeast Alaska. The majority of the baskets are made from spruce roots by Tlingit weavers, from Sitka. There is one basket that is made from red cedar bark, and was done by a Haida weaver. Haida weavers also used spruce root, however.

The Doris Borhauer Basket Collection is owned by the Sitka National Historical Park, and the majority of the time only part of the collection is on display. Most of the collection remains in storage due to limited dis

Many weavers are in this photo of the 1934 Alaska Native Sisterhood Convention.
Photo courtesy of Selina Claggett and Harold Jacobs.

play space and because exposure to light causes the colors of the baskets to fade. The Sitka National Historical Park purchased this collection of baskets from Doris Borhauer, a physical therapist, in 1970 for a very reasonable cost. Mrs. Borhauer acquired a large part of her collection from Lila Berg, who was also in the health-care field.

The idea for this project was generated by Elders of the Sitka Tribe of Alaska. During a conference on native use of plants, the *Haa Kayaaní Conference* in Sitka,

Descendents of weavers, elders, and modern weavers view baskets from the collection during the "Celebration of Weavers" April 15 and 16, 2005.

Alaska, in May of 2001, Elders attending the conference had the opportunity to view the Doris Borhauer Basket Collection. The materials used in basket weaving come from plant matter, so this was an interest to some who attended the conference. Some Elders had mothers, grandmothers, or friends who were weavers of baskets in this collection. At the viewing, they reminisced about how their ancestors would weave, how they collected the spruce roots used in weaving, and how they dyed materials for decoration. This event was used as a basis to write a Historic Preservation grant through the National Park Service, with the purpose of further documenting the basket weavers by interviewing with people who still remember them.

This book is based upon the final report from this project, which was a collection catalog of the baskets and their weavers. The project culminated in a two-day "Celebration of Weavers" that brought together descendents and acquaintances of the weavers from across the state to Sitka. As part of the Celebration, all of the baskets of the Doris Borhauer Basket Collection were put on exhibit for the first time ever, and many were brought out of storage that were seldom seen. The descendants got a chance for a private viewing of the Doris Borhauer Basket Collection, where they were able to see and hold their ancestors' baskets. There was also a public event at the Sitka National Historical Park Visitor Center that honored the weavers. The public got to view the collection, view a historical film on basket weaving, try weaving a basket themselves, and listen to a Tlingit story involving baskets, among other activities.

This project was made possible by the extensive notes that Doris Borhauer kept on every basket in her collection. Mrs. Borhauer noted many details about each basket, including where the basket came from, when it was purchased, and frequently, who wove the basket. Further research could only be done because of these notes. These notes on individual baskets contain the exact words and spellings that Mrs. Borhauer used.

This photo shows the Doris Borhauer Basket Collection, as it was acquired by Sitka National Historical Park in 1970. *Photo courtesy Sitka National Historical Park.*

The following is an article from the *Sitka Sentinel* published when the collection was donated:

Borhauer Basket Collection for Sitka

Tuesday, November 3, 1970

THE DAILY SENT

Photo from the Sitka Sentinel, *November 3, 1970*

In September of this year, Sitka lost a good friend, Mrs. Doris Borhauer; but her friendship for this community will not be forgotten. It was announced today that Mrs. Borhauer's well-known spruce root basket collection has been acquired by the National Park Service and will remain permanently at the Sitka National Monument Visitor Center.

The collection consists of 92 spruce root baskets ranging in sizes from 1 1/4 x 1 1/2 inches to 16 x 17 1/2 inches. They date from 1850 to 1967. All sorts of styles and shapes are represented in the collection and some that were woven especially for sale. The variety of size, shape, and age of the baskets makes the collection extremely significant for illustrating the history of the basket weaver's art. Because spruce root basketry is almost exclusively Tlingit, these baskets are more representative of the aesthetic value of the people than even the totem pole. The designs on the baskets were used by the weaver solely because of their decorative value; while in Tlingit painting and carving, where realistic forms prevail, the totemic significance of the design is all-important.

Mrs. Borhauer came to Sitka in 1956 as physical therapist at the USPHS Hospital. She married her late husband Buster in 1957 and very soon thereafter, she went into private practice as a physical therapist. By doing so, she filled a very real need in the community.

Mrs. Borhauer explained in her own words her reason for collecting spruce root baskets, "My husband and I were very much interested in the history of Alaska and the Alaska native arts and crafts, each of us having acquired a few native items on previous visits. We soon realized the art of spruce root weaving was being kept active by only a few Tlingit women. Thus, the collection of spruce root baskets became our main interest and hobby, which occupied many enlightening and delightful hours of study and travel in southeast Alaska, developed. We were enriched by the warmth of the Tlingit people we met in many small villages and cities. We listened to fascinating Indian legends, were shown old family heirlooms, and were privileged to take pictures of many of them. It was our good fortune to be able to purchase many very old spruce root utility baskets, several of which had been used by three or four generations.

"When Mr. and Mrs. L. C. Berg retired and decided to move to Portland, Buster and I purchased Mrs. Berg's basket collection. It was Mrs. Berg's desire that the spruce root baskets remain in Southeast Alaska where they were woven. My husband and I heartily agreed. It was through my husband's appreciation of this fine art and through his diligent efforts that we were able to fulfill a fascinating hobby and have a part in preserving some of the artistry of spruce root weaving. The Tlingit women of Sitka and of Southeast Alaska, past and present, have contributed to a fine collection of utility and decorative spruce root baskets which will be viewed, enjoyed, and appreciated for years to come."

Thus, at considerable monetary sacrifice to herself, Mrs. Borhauer enabled the National Park Service to acquire these baskets on condition that they remain permanently at Sitka National Monument. Indeed, Doris Borhauer's friendship for Sitka and for Tlingit art will not be forgotten.

Doris Borhauer

Doris Borhauer was born December 11, 1907, in Hibbing, Minnesota, according to her obituary. She was the daughter of Ernest Granville Robie and Lillian Belle Turnbull Robie.

One of Doris' close friends in Sitka was Brownie Thomsen, who worked with her at the Indian Health Service hospital, Mt. Edgecumbe. Brownie shared what she knew about Doris. Doris moved to Sitka in 1956.

Doris was a physical therapist, and worked in different university hospitals in Oregon, Wisconsin, and Illinois before she moved to Sitka to work for Mt. Edgecumbe Hospital. According to her obituary, Doris married Buster Borhauer in Sitka in June 1957. She went into private practice as a physical therapist in 1958. Brownie said Doris had no children. Her obituary from the *Tillamook County Headlight Herald* stated that she was survived by a nephew, Larry Sheridan, and a niece, Lynn Woock.

Brownie remembers Doris as being a very reserved person. Brownie said that Doris was very straightforward,

Doris Borhauer at far right. Also pictured: Shirley Kimball (second from left), her son (left), and her daughter (second from right). *Photo courtesy of Shirley Kimball and Brownie Thomsen.*

and you always knew where you stood with her. Doris was a no-nonsense person, and she didn't joke around, she was serious. Doris was a very active woman, and liked to swim and hike. She taught Brownie how to swim and went swimming every day. Doris was not one to talk about her personal life. Brownie remembered she was very organized, which may be why she kept notes on all the baskets in her collection.

She remembered that Doris had many baskets in the living room of her house on Halibut Point Road, across from the City Shops. Brownie remembered that Doris had a large glass case with baskets in it, though Brownie didn't know much about Doris's basket collection. Brownie didn't remember seeing as many baskets as she had in her collection, so Doris might have had baskets somewhere else besides her living room. Brownie did remember Lila Berg, from whom Doris bought a large part of her collection, but didn't know why Lila sold it. Brownie rememberes that there was a shop at the hospital where patients' families sent baskets to sell, so Doris might have purchased some of her baskets there.

Doris eventually went into private practice for physical therapy and worked part time. Later, she and Buster decided to move to Oregon, however, Buster died before they could leave. Doris moved to Oregon the next year anyway because she could not afford to work part-time in Sitka. Doris thought that her basket collection should remain in Sitka, so she sold it to Sitka National Historical Park for a nominal fee (see newspaper article).

Doris worked at Tillamook County General Hospital from 1970 until her retirement in 1983. Brownie remembers that she came back to Sitka to visit several times after she left. Doris didn't remarry until 1989, when she married Howard McConnell in Tillamook on November 12. Brownie went to see her in Tillamook in 1991. Doris lived in Oregon until the end of her life. Her husband, Howard, died in February 1994. Doris herself died shortly thereafter, August 9, 1994, in Tillamook, Oregon. She was eighty-six years old.

Lila Brougher Berg

Sixty-three of the baskets in the collection were originally purchased or acquired by Lila Brougher Berg, a public health nurse in Sitka during the 1930s through the 1950s. Doris Borhauer knew Lila Berg because they both worked for the Indian Health Service, and Doris purchased part of Lila's collection.

Lila L. Brougher was born in La Center, Washington, in 1897. Lila came to Sitka unmarried, and many of the baskets are noted being purchased by "Lila Brougher" or "L. L. Brougher," which was her maiden name. When Lila first came to Sitka, she lived at Sheldon Jackson School, and taught and nursed there. In the 1930 Census, it is noted that Lila lived at Sheldon Jackson and was a graduate nurse.

Louie and Lila Berg. *Photo courtesy of Margaret Dangel.*

Lila married Ludwig "Louie" Berg, a fish buyer who worked for the cold storage in Sitka. Louie was a widower and had four children, so Lila helped raise his children, and never had any of her own. There were three daughters, Louise, Dorothy, and Ella, and one son, Carl. Margaret Dangel knew Lila, and was friends with her stepdaughter, Louise. Margaret was in the Girl Scouts with all of the girls. Margaret remembers that Lila was active in the Sitka Women's Club and the Girl Scouts. Margaret also remembers, "She had a lot of baskets at her house."

Lila was well known in the native community for the help she gave as a public health nurse, in a time before there were doctors and hospitals. Lila would often trade her services for baskets—one of the baskets in the collection was in payment for helping with the birth of a baby. Lila also taught hygiene, and a number of baskets were traded for a "Home Hygiene textbook." John Bartels, who was a boy growing up in the Sitka Indian Village, remembers Lila as "fearless." She was not afraid to go into a house contaminated with tuberculosis, and explain to the women how to quarantine the sick members of the family.

Jean Boone-Hamar, the daughter of one of the weavers in the collection, remembered Lila. "I remember this Mrs. Berg; she used to come down to the house quite often. She was always so nice and curious. I remember her hair used to always either be back or in a bun or something and I used to wonder, how does she ever keep her hair so nice?" Jean remembered Lila teaching people in the Sitka Indian Village about hygiene. "The people had a meeting in the village, and I was very young at the time. . . . They gathered around and [said] anybody who has cracked dishes in their house, . . . throw them away because somebody told them, and I don't know if it was Mrs. Berg, that it is not good to eat with dishes with cracks in it, because there's germs in it that will make you sick. And you know before that we probably just used them and never thought about anything about a cracked dish. . . . Now you know when you use a cracked dish you don't use it because there's germs gathering in it."

Lila and Louie moved down to the Portland area in the late 1930s to be near Louie's children who were going to school there. Lila and Louie moved back to Sitka "after the girls got settled," Margaret said. They eventually moved back to Portland in the 1960s. Louie Berg died in July 1969 in Oregon. Lila remarried after Louie died. She married Clarke "Fred" Coulson, and remained married to him until the end of her life. Lila and Fred both died in January 1983. Lila was eighty-six years old.

◻ Historical Perspective

Many of the baskets in this collection were woven and sold from the turn of the twentieth century through the 1960s, although there are some from the 1800s. This was a time when basket weavers started selling baskets made specifically for the tourist market. Baskets were not made as much for utilitarian purposes like cooking and holding berries or other goods. Maria Guthrie said, "The very early years it was a survival technique, keeping your home going, making these [baskets] for use. At that time, . . . when [my mother] was growing up, a lot of [the baskets were] not sold. It was survival use." The native people had access to metal pots that were superior for cooking compared to baskets. In the earlier part of the 1900s, some people did still make and use berrying baskets, but even these were gradually replaced by other containers.

Instead, as the Tlingit people started to integrate into the western Christian society, they started to make fancy baskets made to sell to tourists. The native people sold these first to supplement their traditional foods—to pay for staples like flour, rice, and sugar while they still gathered berries and plants and hunted and fished. One of the basket types that was frequently sold to tourists was the spruce root rattle-top basket. This type existed before Western contact, but grew popular when more baskets with fancy designs began to be sold. Weavers also made baskets without lids, with the traditional geometric native designs, and with more anthromorphic designs like killer whales or birds and flowers.

One of the people interviewed for this project, Irene Jimmy, remembered the proficiency of the weavers. "During [my mother's] generation, there were quite a few skilled weavers of spruce root here in Sitka. In her generation, that's what they used. In my generation, we used cedar bark. They took a lot of pride in their workmanship. They were very competitive among each other in her generation. I think that . . . resulted in

Native Women Weaving Baskets, Sitka, Alaska. Copyright 1897. *Photo by Winter and Pond: Alaska State Library/ Winter and Pond. Photographs, ca. 1893–1943/87-0106.*

Native street scene, Sitka, Alaska. *Photo by Case and Draper: Alaska State Library/Case and Draper. Photographs, ca. 1898–1920/P39-0176*

these beautiful baskets that you see now in Sitka. A lot of it had to do with preparation. From what I saw of my mother's materials, she took great care and took the time to split the roots."

A large part of the baskets in this collection was made for the tourist trade, and these baskets were made by Sitka Tlingit weavers. Sitka had a booming tourist trade from steamships that visited beginning at the turn of the twentieth century through the 1950s. Native women from the Indian village (then called the *Ranche* from a Russian term) would set up blankets or tables to sell their wares on the main thoroughfare (Lincoln Street) where the steamships disembarked, and later where the seaplanes disembarked. They sold their handicrafts, especially beaded moccasins, beaded barrettes, baskets, and even berries.

Several of the people interviewed remembered how the weavers or their children would take little red wagons from the Indian Village to Lincoln Street full of the handicrafts, and that they would set up on sidewalks once they got there. Jean Boone-Hamar, daughter of one of the weavers, recalled, "I used to take all the things that we made down across from the Pioneer Home and set up a little table and sell all the things that we made during the winter. They were mostly baskets, and then there'd be little pins or little barrettes, . . . anything beaded.... I always sold everything. In those days, when I sold those baskets, I think the highest one may have been sold for twenty-five dollars, and they were big with . . . a lid on it."

Beaded footwear and baskets for sale on a steamship dock. *Photo: Alaska State Library/Alaska State Library Place File/Petersburg-People-01*

WEAVERS

(alphabetical order)

>> Mrs. Annie Andrews

BIOGRAPHY

Mrs. Annie Andrews was married to Alex Andrews, a leader of the Kaagwaantaan Clan. They lived in the Eagle's Nest House on Katlian Street in the Sitka Indian Village. According to Harold Jacobs, Annie was the daughter of Arthur and Annie Stevens. She was T'akdeintaan from the Snail House in Hoonah, and her Tlingit name was *Syaanjín*.

Mrs. Annie Andrews. *Photo courtesy of Jean Boone-Hamar.*

Mr. and Mrs. Andrews adopted Jean Andrews (now Jean Boone-Hamar) and raised her in Sitka from the age of three years. Annie and Alex did have one biological son that Jean knew of named Thomas, who died in the 1940s. They adopted other children, which is a tradition in the native culture, and also raised Esther Samboy, who lives in Washington. Annie and Alex spoke very little English and mostly spoke Tlingit, which is what Jean grew up speaking. Mrs. Andrews signed her name with an X.

Mrs. Andrews had a sister, Jenny Anderson (Tlingit name *Shkáal.aat*), and they lived on a fox farm when they were young. Jean Boone-Hamar said, "They used to love to be on the fox farm." Jean thought that the fox farm was on Chichagof Island. They probably stopped raising foxes when the price of furs went down. Mrs. Andrews' sister had several children: Esther, Hazel, George, Helen, and Lawrence Anderson. George Anderson and Esther (now Ricaporte) are still alive, and they both live in Sitka.

Mrs. Andrews had a physical disability and had a problem with one leg, so she couldn't walk for long distances or any length of time. Alex used to help her gather spruce roots, even though that was "women's work." Jean remembers they would go out to near their fish camp on Halleck Island to harvest roots.

Jean remembers Mrs. Andrews weaving. "Yes, I remember my mother doing the basket weaving for hours. She'd get up and she'd do it from the time she got up to the time she went to bed. She was very good at it. . . . They did it all traditional. I can't remember all the dyes they used to use, but they'd . . . pull some roots and cook them down and then we'd submerge a whole bunch of spruce roots in it."

Jean said they wove primarily to make some extra cash. "The money that my mom brought in for basket weaving bought us staples like sugar and milk and things like that . . . My mom and dad were always working. . . . Our meat in our household was always fish or dear meat." Jean said that, "we never kept any of our work. I never remember it on the shelf. . . . We always sold, and they all sold, every one of them. I don't know how many she did, but she used to do a lot in one winter, just continuous, working all the time."

Mrs. Andrews taught Jean how to weave, and they both sold their baskets to tourists from the steamships that came to Sitka. Jean said, "there used to be tons of tourists. . . ." One of Jean's baskets is in the collection, woven when she was twelve years old (see Jean Andrews Boone-Hamar's biography). Mrs. Andrews also made beaded moccasins and other beaded items to sell. Jean talked about selling to the tourists, and that she would go to the main street to sell to the tourists since her mother was disabled. "I used to take all the things that we made down . . . across from the Pioneer Home and set up a little table and sell all the things we made during the winter. . . . I always sold everything."

Jean said she was a teenager, around fifteen years old, when Mrs. Andrews died in 1959.

Baskets: Annie Andrews is the weaver with the most baskets in the Doris Borhauer Collection (a total of ten). Her baskets have been noted by some for having "M&M" colors, the colors of the old M&M candies with brown, orange, green, yellow, and tan.

National Park Service Catalog No. 669

YEAR MADE: 1956   YEAR OBTAINED: 1956

Doris Borhauer's Notes: This small spruce root basket was made by Mrs. Alex (Annie) Andrews, a Sitka Thlingit Indian woman, using roots gathered in the spring of 1956—woven in September 1956 and purchased by Mrs. Lila Berg who watched her weave.

Previous owner: Lila Brougher Berg

National Park Service Catalog No. 671

YEAR MADE: 1958   YEAR OBTAINED: 1959

Doris Borhauer's Notes: This lovely, small spruce root basket was made by Mrs. Alex (Annie) Andrews, a Sitka Thlingit Indian woman, in 1958 and presented to Mrs. Lila Berg as a Russian Christmas gift.

Previous owner: Lila Brougher Berg

National Park Service Catalog No. 678

YEAR MADE: 1958   YEAR OBTAINED: 1958

Doris Borhauer's Notes: This spruce root basket was made by Mrs. Alex (Annie) Andrews, a Sitka Thlingit Indian woman, in September 1958, and purchased that year by Mrs. L. C. Berg.

Previous owner: Lila Brougher Berg

National Park Service Catalog No. 697

YEAR MADE: 1956   YEAR OBTAINED: 1956

Doris Borhauer's Notes: This spruce root basket was made by Mrs. Alex (Annie) Andrews, a Sitka Thlingit Indian woman, in 1956. The dye in the pattern is native and made by Mrs. Andrews' mother, Mrs. Stevens. Purchased in 1956 by Lila Berg.

Previous owner: Lila Brougher Berg

National Park Service Catalog No. 698

YEAR MADE: 1957

Doris Borhauer's Notes: This spruce root basket was made by Mrs. Alex (Annie) Andrews in July 1957. Made of roots gathered that spring. Mr. Andrews and daughter Jean assisted in gathering the roots. The Andrews are Sitka Thlingit Indians.

National Park Service Catalog No. 704

YEAR MADE: 1957   YEAR OBTAINED: 1957

Doris Borhauer's Notes: This spruce root basket was made by Mrs. Alex (Annie) Andrews, a Sitka Thlingit Indian woman, in 1957. The roots were gathered in the spring of 1957 and the design made of the stem of maidenhair fern. Purchased the same year by Mrs. L. C. Berg.

Note for basket No. 704: Although this design is known today by some as a swastika, a symbol of the Nazis, it is also an ancient Native American symbol which meant good fortune. This design was also used by the Tlingit.

Previous owner: Lila Brougher Berg

15

National Park Service Catalog No. 705

YEAR MADE: 1959

Doris Borhauer's Notes: This spruce root basket was made in 1959 by Mrs. Alex (Annie) Andrews. She was an expert weaver and I had the privilege to watch her weave several baskets. This was one of the last she made before she died in August 1959. The rose and green of the design are probably diamond dye.

National Park Service Catalog No. 721

YEAR OBTAINED: 1957

Doris Borhauer's Notes: This covered spruce root basket was made by Mrs. Alex (Annie) Andrews, a Sitka Thlingit Indian woman, and it was entered in the Sitka community Fair of 1957 and received second prize, cash and a red ribbon. Purchased in fall of 1957 by Lila Berg.

Previous owner: Lila Brougher Berg

National Park Service Catalog No. 711

YEAR MADE: 1956   YEAR OBTAINED: 1965

Doris Borhauer's Notes: This spruce root basket was made by Mrs. Alex (Annie) Andrews, a Sitka Thlingit Indian woman, of roots gathered the last week of July 1956. The green dye of the grass pattern was prepared by Mrs. Andrew's mother, Mrs. Stevens, of Sitka cottages many years ago. Purchased by Lila Berg August 16, 1965.

Previous owner: Lila Brougher Berg

National Park Service Catalog No. 731

YEAR MADE: 1956   YEAR OBTAINED: 1956

Doris Borhauer's Notes: This covered spruce root basket was made in 1956 by Mrs. Alex (Annie) Andrews, a Sitka Thlingit Indian woman. This pattern was copied from a basket owned by Mrs. Caroline Yaw of Sitka, Alaska. Buckshot rattles in lid. Purchased in 1956 by Lila Berg.

Previous owner: Lila Brougher Berg

>> Ms. Jean Andrews Boone-Hamar

BIOGRAPHY

Jean Andrews Boone-Hamar is the adopted daughter of Annie and Alex Andrews, and her maiden name was Jean Andrews. Mrs. Boone-Hamar originally came from Angoon, but was raised by Alex and Annie as their own from the age of three. She is a T'akdeintaan, or Raven Sea Pigeon, like her mother Annie. Jean remarked her godmother was Mrs. Hoolis (Lily Hoolis John), who is another weaver of baskets in the collection.

Alex and Annie spoke Tlingit, and very little English, so Jean grew up speaking Tlingit, though she says she's lost the language now. Jean said, "I can remember coming in and them telling my mom not to talk Tlingit to me, in the forties." Jean grew up in the Eagle's Nest Clan house. Her father, Alex, was a

Jean and her father Alex Andrews. *Photo courtesy Jean Boone-Hamar.*

leader of the Kaagwaantaan. Her parents were elderly when they adopted her; her father received social security. Her mother died when Jean was just fifteen years old.

Annie, her mother, taught Jean how to weave when she was a young girl. The basket in this collection was woven when Jean was twelve years old. Jean talked about learning to weave: "They made us, if we didn't do it right, we'd have to rip it out. I'd have to rip it out and redo it. Yes, [my mother] was a very good teacher."

Annie sold both their baskets to the tourists. Jean says she never got to keep her baskets, because they needed to sell them for staples like rice, flour, and sugar, things they didn't get from the land. All other food they got by hunting, fishing, and gathering. The family had a fish camp on Halleck Island, north of Sitka, in Nakwasina Sound.

Jean said her parents worked hard all of the time, always gathering food, or making crafts to sell in the winter, and that they lived a frugal life. "I can remember going back to school in September and the teachers saying, write down all the fun you had this year, and I used to say, they don't know how hard the children in the village work. We work as soon as school is out, we go to . . . fish camp and they catch fish. Even the small kids, if they can carry, they do that."

Jean is grateful to have been raised by her parents, Annie and Alex. She said, "They taught me everything. They brought me from Angoon . . . to Sitka, which I'm glad. Otherwise I wouldn't have gotten educated, so I feel fortunate in that."

Jean as a girl in regalia. *Photo courtesy Jean Boone-Hamar.*

National Park Service Catalog No. 670

YEAR MADE: 1956   YEAR OBTAINED: 1956

Doris Borhauer's Notes: This spruce root basket was the second one made by twelve-year-old Jean Andrews (foster child of Mr. and Mrs. Alex Andrews)—a Thlingit Indian born in Juneau, Alaska. Her father was Charlie Walter. Made in July 1956—and made in two days. She learned how to dig the roots and prepare them. Purchased in September 1956 by Lila Berg.

Previous owner: Lila Brougher Berg

❯❯ Mrs. Nellie Aragon

Biography

Mrs. Nellie Aragon was born Nellie Williams, the daughter of Mary Williams. She was married three times: to a man named Coulter, to Miguel Salas Aragon (at the time the basket was made), and to Max Lindoff. Mrs. Aragon had an adopted son, William Aragon, and had no other children. She does have some grandchildren, including David, Steven, and Billie Aragon. Her occupation was listed as being a cannery worker, and she also listed that she sold handcrafts.

Bob Sam remembers that Mrs. Aragon was one of his grandmother's friends, who would come over to have lunch and weave with other Native ladies. Bob remembers that he would help Mrs. Aragon take her handicrafts downtown to sell to tourists, after he had helped his grandmother.

Harold Jacobs provided information that her Tlingit name was Shaḵéiwés and that she was from the Koosk'eidí Clan, from the Cow House.

Nellie Aragon. *Photo by Martin Strand. Kettleson Memorial Library/ Romaine Hardcastle Collection/ RHC01-046-9c*

BASKET ON NEXT PAGE.

National Park Service Catalog No. 717

YEAR MADE: 1932   YEAR OBTAINED: 1932

Doris Borhauer's Notes: This spruce root basket was made by Mrs. Nellie Aragon, a Sitka Thlingit Indian woman, in 1932. Purchased from her by Miss L. L. Brougher, government nurse, 1932.

Previous owner: Lila Brougher Berg

>> Mrs. Katherine Benson

BIOGRAPHY

Mrs. Katherine Benson was married to Charles Benson. Mrs. Benson wove spruce root baskets. One of her daughters is Irene Jimmy, who is also a weaver of spruce root baskets, Chilkat, and Ravenstail.

Mrs. Benson was a Kiks.ádi lady, from the Steel House (*Shteen Hít*), according to Harold Jacobs. Her Tlingit name was *Kookáxk'w*. Mr. Jacobs noted that her father was Archie Wanamaker (Tlingit name *Yashgeit Éesh*), a Wooshkeetaan, and her mother was Katherine Wanamaker (Tlingit name *Yankawgei*).

Mrs. Benson was born in 1886, and lived until she was eighty, dying in 1966. Mrs. Benson had eight children altogether. She was married to another man before Mr. Benson, and had two daughters. Then she married Charles Benson and had four sons and Irene. One of her sons was Henry Benson.

Irene says that her mother was "a very quiet person, very reserved. Just really cared a lot about her family. She really treasured her grandchildren. . . . As I grew up I don't recall her ever being very angry at anyone. And she never, even when they got angry with her, she never . . . responded the same way."

Mrs. Katherine Benson. *Photo from Irene Jimmy, given to SNHP.*

Irene says her mother was active in the Alaska Native Sisterhood and the Sitka Historical Society. She also participated in native dance groups in the 1940s. She also liked to dance, "no matter what kind of form it was. . . . I remember my dad and mom used to go dancing at the ANB Hall when they [had] those social[s]." Mrs. Benson also made regalia for the native dance groups.

Irene remembers her mother weaving: "I think about this and how her fingers would fly through the weft . . . how straight [her weaving] is. . . . I could still see her sitting in the corner hour after hour weaving on her basket and being very careful with it. She never left her baskets or material out in the open. She always covered them when she was not working with them."

Mrs. Benson had a great deal of skill weaving baskets, and [she] wove with fine roots. Mrs. Benson used cardboard on the bottom, cut round to fit and sewn on to protect the bottom of her baskets. Irene said, "From what I saw [of] my mother's materials, she took great care and took the time to split the roots, looking at her baskets. . . . They were all fine roots, they were not the bigger size. She enjoyed the fine roots."

Mrs. Benson did not teach Irene to weave because Irene was away at Sheldon Jackson Boarding School. "Her goal was to have me learn the Christian culture. I guess she knew that's where it was going to be." Delores Churchill taught Irene to weave, after Irene's mother died. Irene's daughter, Karen Kane, is also a weaver, and Irene has taught her granddaughter Jennifer to weave. So even though Mrs. Benson did not teach anyone to weave, the tradition lives on in her family.

National Park Service Catalog No. 690

YEAR MADE: 1957   YEAR OBTAINED: 1957

Doris Borhauer's Notes: This lovely spruce root basket with a braided handle was made by Mrs. Charles Benson, a Sitka Thlingit Indian woman, in February 1957. Purchased that year by Lila Berg.

Previous owner: Lila Brougher Berg

>> Mrs. Lydia Charles

BIOGRAPHY

Lydia Charles was married to Powell Charles. They had thirteen children, according to her granddaughter Erna Fawcett, and only seven survived a smallpox epidemic. Erna's father, Lee Charles, was Mrs. Charles's son. Other children who survived were Norman, Gibson, Melvin, and Paul Charles. Nelson Frank, a relation of Mrs. Charles's through his father's side, who grew up in Hydaburg where Mrs. Charles lived, said that her last living son, Norman, died recently in Ketchikan at age eighty-eight.

According to Nelson, Mrs. Charles was half Haida; her mother was Haida and her father was a sailing captain. Mrs. Charles was from the Double-headed Eagle Clan, her granddaughter Erna said. Nelson said that Mrs. Charles grew up in Kasaan, and moved to Klinkwan when she married Powell Charles. They moved to Hydaburg in 1926.

Mrs. Charles's granddaughter, Erna, remembers that her grandmother wove baskets, made blankets, and carved. Mrs. Charles encouraged Erna to participate in traditional dancing, and made her regalia for the dance shows.

Nelson Frank remembers Mrs. Charles weaving with other ladies in Hydaburg. "They had a weaving

Lydia Charles with her husband, Powell, and children: Powell, Leonard, Norman, and Lee. *Photo courtesy of Nelson Frank.*

circle in Hydaburg, made up of about ten to twenty of the women. And each time they had a meeting, it was in somebody else's house. They'd just bring their material there and sit down and talk and tell stories. [Mrs. Charles] was kind of a leader in making hats. She knew how to make hats. They'd consult her, and she'd help them shape it." Nelson learned to weave himself by observing the group of weavers. "I learned from these ladies. . . . I used to enjoy their stories when they'd start on an object. They'd describe it to everyone, and what they intend to do with it. If there's any change, then the people would [say,] 'No, I wouldn't do [it] like that, it would make it look too puffy,' and then they'd change it and go back."

Nelson thinks highly of Mrs. Charles's weaving. "She was the best hat weaver and the best weaver in the bunch. . . . Mrs. Charles made a lot of hats. That was probably her big forté. Then she made a lot of carrying baskets, like we'd [have] a packsack today." Nelson also said, "It's amazing to me to look at some of the things she made for her own family, for example. It wasn't any more superior quality than the stuff she [sold] on the street. Same, no change. . . . It shows me that somebody has a high discipline."

Mrs. Charles's granddaughter Erna said Mrs. Charles passed away in 1974, and she was in her seventies. As the baskets in this collection were made in 1967, she made them late in life.

National Park Service Catalog No. 745

YEAR MADE: 1967   YEAR OBTAINED: 1967

Doris Borhauer's Notes: This spruce root basket with open weave above and below center design and with rattle in lid was made by Mrs. Lydia Charles, Hydaburg, Alaska, in August 1967. Purchased September 1967.

National Park Service Catalog No. 746

YEAR MADE: 1967   YEAR OBTAINED: 1967

Doris Borhauer's Notes: This small spruce root basket with rattle in lid was made by Mrs. Lydia Charles, Hydaburg, Alaska, in August 1967. Purchased September 1967.

National Park Service Catalog No. 747

YEAR MADE: 1967   YEAR OBTAINED: 1967

Doris Borhauer's Notes: This spruce root basket woven in shape of iron kettle was made by Mrs. Lydia Charles, Hydaburg, Alaska, in August 1967. Purchased September 1967.

>> Mrs. Christine Davis

BIOGRAPHY

Mrs. Christine Davis was married to Peter Davis. Herman Davis remembers Christine Davis, because she was his Uncle Peter's wife. Herman knew very little about her, other than that he met her once, and that Mrs. Davis had no children.

Records from the 1930 Census, around the time that the basket in this collection was made, list Peter Davis (thirty-seven years old) and his wife Christine (thirty-seven years old, born in 1893) as living in Juneau,

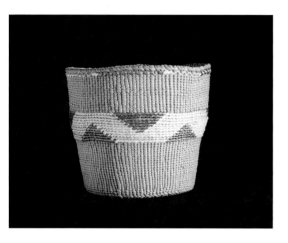

Alaska. The census lists Peter as a fisherman, and Christine as a cannery worker. It also lists their son, Weldon, as being three and a half years old. A search for Weldon Davis listed a man by that name as having died in the Korean Conflict, so it is possible their son died in the 1950s.

National Park Service Catalog No. 676

YEAR MADE: 1931   YEAR OBTAINED: 1931

Doris Borhauer's Notes: This spruce root basket was made by Mrs. Christine (Peter) Davis, a Sitka Thlingit Indian woman, in May 1931 to pay nurse Lila L. Brougher for her home hygiene textbook.

Previous owner: Lila Brougher Berg

>> Mrs. Kitty Dawson

BIOGRAPHY

Little is known about Mrs. Kitty Dawson. No one contacted in Sitka knew of her, and the only Dawson listed in census records in 1920 was George Dawson (ninety-one years old) and his wife Flora (sixty-five years old). It is possible that this might have been the same woman. Also, in the Russian Cemetery, there

is a headstone with the name Mrs. Katie Dawson. This might possibly be the weaver, since both Kitty and Katie are derivatives of Katherine. Also, in the Russian Orthodox Church, most people had different church names, so the different names may be the same person.

National Park Service Catalog No. 677

YEAR MADE: CIRCA 1930

YEAR OBTAINED: 1940

Doris Borhauer's Notes: This spruce root basket was made by Mrs. Kitty Dawson, a Thlingit Indian woman of Sitka, Alaska about 1930. Purchased in 1940 by Lila Berg.

Previous owner: Lila Brougher Berg

>> Mrs. Katherine Dimitri

BIOGRAPHY

Mrs. Katherine Dimitri (spelled Demetrie by Mrs. Borhauer) was married to Tom Dimitri, who was of the Chookaneidí Clan. She was originally of the Ľeeneidí Clan from Juneau, but was adopted into the Ľuknax̱.ádi in Sitka, according to Bob Sam, who said that his family is closely related to her. Bob said that after his mother moved to Sitka from Juneau, her baby sister Rachel was sent to Sitka to live with Mrs. Dimitri, because the rest of Rachel's family had died of tuberculosis. Bob said, "When my mother married my father, Mrs. Dimitri took [Rachel] in as one of her own children." Mrs. Dimitri took care of Rachel like her own child until Rachel died of tuberculosis too, and she was buried in the Dimitri family plot.

Katherine Dimitri from 1934 ANS photo. *Photo courtesy of Harold Jacobs.*

According to Bessie Kitka, Bob's mother, Mrs. Katherine Dimitri's sister was Lilly Hoolis John, another basket weaver in this collection. Mrs. Dimitri's Tlingit name was *Neilyoodusheet*, and she was from the Dog Salmon House of the Auke people, according to Harold Jacobs.

Bob remembers that Mrs. Dimitri wove baskets and sold them to tourists, as his grandmother did. Bob would help Mrs. Dimitri take her crafts down to the main street to sell in the same way he helped his grandmother. "I would take my grandmother's wagon down there first, and set it all up and get it ready for her to come down. Then I'd run down and get Mrs. Dimitri's. . . . I really enjoyed doing that because they paid me fifty cents. . . ."

Bob talked about Mrs. Dimitri's house. "[Mrs. Dimitri] had the only house in the village . . . with the bear in front of it, [the] marble bear. She had the only house in the village that had a fence around it. So it was used as [a] barrier for the all the kids. And when all the parents were going downtown for shopping or whatever, they'd drop us off in the fence there and we had to stay there until they came back. Mrs. Dimitri would watch us."

National Park Service Catalog No. 710

YEAR MADE: CA. 1880

Doris Borhauer's Notes: This old spruce root tray was made by Mrs. Demetrie about 1880 and used by her to cook blueberries in. Later she used it to hold beads or buttons as she sewed or trimmed moccasins. She was a Thlingit Indian and an Aunt of Mary Williams (Mrs. Cyrus Williams), from whom Lila Berg obtained the basket.

Previous owner: Lila Brougher Berg

>> Mrs. Lucy Frank

BIOGRAPHY

Lucy Frank was a Haida woman from Massett, British Columbia, of the Eagle Hummingbird Clan. Her daughter, Mona Jackson, is still alive at the age of ninety-four. Mona's daughter, Della Cheney, was interviewed for this project. Selina Peratrovich, another Haida weaver in this collection, was a niece of Mrs.

Frank. Mrs. Frank's maiden name was Jones, and she first married Benjamin Ingram. After her first husband died, she married Luke Frank, who became stepfather to her children. She had seven children with her first husband, Benjamin, and Luke had five children, so they had twelve children all together.

Many of these children, six or eight, died of tuberculosis, and Mrs. Frank cared for them all through it. Della said, "She was very strong-minded." She was very insistent that her children go to school, and sent Mona to Sheldon Jackson School in Sitka. After Mona finished at Sheldon Jackson, her mother wanted her to go to college so she could be a teacher, and she graduated with a bachelor of science degree from Ashville Normal School for Women in 1939. Della said, "[Mona's] mother was very influential in her life."

Mrs. Frank spoke mostly Haida, so Della didn't understand much of what she said. Della's mother, Mona, often translated for her. Mona kept her Haida language even though she went off to school where she couldn't speak it, "because she loved her mother so much." Della said that she would talk to her mother in her mind in Haida.

Lucy Frank with one of her baskets. *Photo courtesy of Della Cheney. Photo also printed in book* This is Haida.

Mrs. Frank might have taught a few of her daughters to weave, but Mona did not get to learn because she was away at school in the winters, when her mother wove. Mona did go out to collect materials when she was home in the summer. One of her sisters wove basket bottoms, and then her mother would weave the sides and finish them. Several of [Mrs. Frank's] grandchildren in Massett are weavers, and Mona and Della later learned how to weave as well. Della remembers that her mother learned to weave when she was almost eighty, and knew she was going blind, so she wove three or four baskets quickly. She couldn't put down her weaving, so her husband fed her.

Della herself learned to weave in 1993 from her cousin Delores Churchill. She says, "Now I'm a full-time, not a full-time weaver, but I work and weave. I guess I work to weave." Della also says, "Now that I've been weaving . . . I have probably learned more from that, than all the years of college [that] I struggled through to get my degree from college. That's a powerful educator, because when we take the time to learn our way of life that is something that is probably the most precious, the most self-loving."

Other descendents of Mrs. Frank also learned to weave. Mona's children who have learned to weave are Norman, Katherine (Jada), Larry, Michael, Gary, and Joel. Other grandchildren who have learned to weave are Gail and Elizabeth Cheney, Dawn Jackson, Mona Evan, and Henry Smith Jr. Mrs. Frank has left quite a legacy of weavers. Della noted, "We did not speak directly to Naani Lucy because she spoke only Haida, but since we have learned to weave, we speak with her constantly. By that, I mean we know when to harvest, process, and practice the weaving techniques she used."

Della has some of her grandmother's baskets in her collection, and also a few baskets that her great-great-great-grandmother had woven, who was blind. So indeed, the family has an impressive lineage of weavers. Della has a cooking basket and a storage basket from her great-great-great-grandmother. The storage basket has part of spruce roots woven upside down, because she didn't realize they were the wrong way since she was blind until someone told her.

Della remembers going out with her grandmother and mother to collect cedar bark when she visited Massett on Haida Gwaii (the Queen Charlotte Islands). The following is Della's story:

> I was telling [my mother] last time I was home that now that I'm a weaver, I know my grandmother very well, because I harvest and process and weave. I know her now better than ever, because if she was here, if she had taught me how to weave, this is the way I would have learned. I was lucky enough to go with her when she was like eighty-four years old, I went to Massett with my mother, and she wanted to go harvest bark, because I was there. Maybe that's when [Grandma Lucy]

planted the seed in my mind that I had to weave. But I didn't know it then, I was younger. That was when I was just getting out of high school, I think, in the sixties . . . I went down there, and we went out to that place. We went there and she started to show us how to find the right tree, and how to start cutting into the bark, and then how to start lifting the bark up off the tree, and it went way up real fast when she took it from me. I was being very gentle, and she took it from me, and she just like shaking out a wet towel, started to move that bark, you know it was about six or eight inches wide. Then it went up high; it must have went up maybe thirty-five feet or so on that one tree. Of course, how do you get it down was my question.

Mother asked her in Haida and she said, she started to twist it, and she pulled down really hard on it, and it didn't break off, of course, the first time. So we changed our position on the ground from standing near the tree, we moved out, farther to the right side or left. And then she twisted it some more. Then she gave it to me because I was younger and stronger, is what my mother told me. So I did what she did, I pulled on it really hard. You have to do it real quick, kind of snap it off. But it didn't break. Grandma—she was looking at me, smiling. She reached over for it. Next thing we knew she was on the other side of the tree. [Della laughed.] She had swung on the bark. And she was old you know! And she swung from that side of the tree to the other side of the tree. It didn't break! She was small, she must have been, when we were out there she must have been around five feet, if that, stretching it. . . . and she must have weighed about maybe one hundred pounds. . . . She was real short and small. She swung, and she had this funny face on her when she got to the other side, looking at me. And then she started twisting at it again and then she snapped it really hard.

I just remember it was like a ribbon, the cedar bark was coming out of the sky, towards us. She said something in Haida, and mother said, 'Move!' [I] got out of the way just in time because it came down right towards me. [Della paused to laugh in memory.]

That was really something. Then she started taking the outer bark out, you know, like she was hand washing something. I remember that pretty clearly because I was really watching her, because she had swung on it for one thing. I didn't think she'd do that. So she had gotten my attention, all right. But, she had a sense of humor that was very spontaneous.

Mrs. Frank died in the mid-1970s, and she was very old. Della thought she was 102 when she passed away, but Nelson Frank, her grandson, thought she was 106.

Della asked her mother about the basket being sold. It was sold in Kake, and purchased from Kadake's Gift Shop. Mrs. Frank left Massett to come visit her daughter Mona in Kake. At the time, they didn't have enough money to send her back, so Mona sold the basket, which her mother had given to her as a gift, to Louise Kadake, who ran the shop. Around the same time, other baskets by Haida weavers were sold in Kake: one by Selina Peratrovich, Mrs. Frank's niece, and another by Agnes Williams, another Haida weaver in Massett. Della thought it was possible that her grandmother might have brought their baskets to Kake with her to sell.

National Park Service Catalog No. 733

YEAR MADE: CA. 1959
YEAR OBTAINED: 1964

Doris Borhauer's Notes: This spruce root basket (small, round with lid) was made at Massett, British Columbia, about 1959 by Mrs. Frank, mother of Mona Frank Jackson (Mrs. Thomas Jackson) of Kake, Alaska. Native dye was used in the grass and root designs. It was purchased at Mrs. Kadake's Curio Store at Kake, Alaska, by Mrs. L. C. Berg May 20, 1964.

Previous owner: Lila Brougher Berg

>> Mrs. Justina "Stella" Jackson

BIOGRAPHY

Justina Jackson, better known as Stella Jackson, was the mother of Daisy Peters. LaVerne Peters is Stella's granddaughter through Daisy Peters. LaVerne now lives in the Pioneer Home, and remembers a little about her grandmother. It is likely that Stella was from the Eagle Moiety, and might have been from the Eagle's Nest House of the Kaagwaantaan. LaVerne has a picture of her mother in regalia with a close friend, dressed in Eagle's Nest House regalia, and they might have been clan sisters. Harold Jacobs noted that her Tlingit name was *Kaajoobéin*.

Stella Jackson from 1934 ANS photo. *Courtesy of Harold Jacobs.*

LaVerne remembered a particular picture she had of her grandmother Stella, where she was wearing a blue dress, and had her hair in a tight bun. LaVerne knew that her grandmother used to make regalia. "I know I got a blanket from her. It has buttons all around."

LaVerne remembers her grandmother made moccasins and baskets. LaVerne said, "I remember she used to weave baskets." LaVerne remembers that the decorations on the baskets were made from dyed grass. LaVerne never learned to weave. She remembers that they would visit her grandmother in the Sitka Indian Village. Stella lived across from the Kitkas in a gray house on Katlian Street. LaVerne thought her grandmother lived a long time, perhaps until she was one hundred years old. LaVerne said she learned some Tlingit words from her, like the words for water and stove.

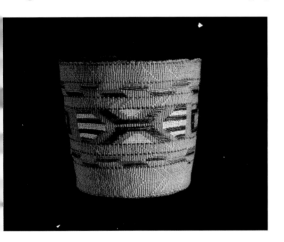

National Park Service Catalog No. 695

YEAR MADE: 1948   YEAR OBTAINED: 1948

Doris Borhauer's Notes: This spruce root basket was made by Mrs. Stella Jackson (mother of Mrs. Richard Peters (Daisy) in 1948. She was a Sitka Thlingit Indian woman. Purchased from Mrs. Jackson by Mrs. L. C. Berg in fall of 1948.

Previous owner: Lila Brougher Berg

>> Mrs. Agnes Jacobs Bellinger

BIOGRAPHY

Agnes Thlunaut Jacobs Bellinger was one of two weavers alive at the time of the project, and she attended the "Celebration of Weavers." She was married to Leo Jacobs Sr. at the time she made the basket. Agnes later married Donal Carroll Bellinger, and is now known as Agnes Bellinger. Agnes lived in Haines, Alaska, where the basket was purchased, until 1969, and then she moved to Juneau.

Agnes was Kaagwaantaan (Eagle-Wolf) and she was born in 1928. Agnes came from the Sitka Wolf House, and was appointed a few years ago to be the

Agnes Bellinger in a Chilkat robe. *Photo courtesy of Mrs. Bellinger's daughter.*

Naa Tlaa (clan mother) of the Chilkat branch of the Sitka Wolf House. Agnes said, "Our grandmothers came from the Wolf House in Sitka. They got married to the men up in Klukwan in the early 1890s."

Agnes was the daughter of Jennie Marks Thlunaut, a renowned Chilkat and basket weaver from Klukwan. Agnes was visually impaired her whole life, but her mother still taught her to weave Chilkat borders, and how to weave baskets. Agnes only ever wove two spruce root baskets, so this basket is indeed rare. Agnes talked about how her mother taught her to harvest spruce roots too. "My mother taught me, like how to harvest the roots and what not, how to prepare it. Of course I can't split the roots now, but I can harvest it and cook it." Agnes also talked about her first basket. "You should see the first one I made. It was all out of shape. My mother use[d] a bear's tooth to smooth it, you know. She put it on a little tiny mason jar, and she rubbed it and rubbed it and rubbed it with the bear's tooth, and it kind of straightened out. It was all out of shape."

Agnes also talked about one of her grandmothers weaving baskets. "I had an auntie, no she was a grandma. She was completely blind, and she put the black colored grass that they used for decoration— you see the red and black decoration on the baskets? She put the black in salt water in a bowl, and she put the red in sugar water in a bowl. That's how she could tell which is red and which is black. [She'd taste it] . . . and she still wove. She still made baskets until she died. She was completely blind."

Agnes sold one of her baskets to a stranger in Haines, and another one to her friend who ran a tourist shop in Haines, Helen Fenn (which is the basket in this collection). Agnes made many different kinds of crafts; she knitted and she used to bead. She made moccasins and purses, and had her own shop for a while, and her friend Helen helped her. Agnes went back to college when she was fifty years old, and got a bachelor of arts degree in cultural anthropology from the University of Washington. Agnes taught the Tlingit language, singing, and dancing. She said, "Now . . . in Klukwan, we're getting all our information together, and we're going to put it on CDs. Everything we can learn, everything about our culture, everything we can put together, because I'm the oldest person from Klukwan now."

Agnes died at her home in Juneau on February 14, 2006, at the age of seventy-eight. She was known accross Alaska for her work preserving the Tligit language and teaching traditional singing and dancing.

National Park Service Catalog No. 741

YEAR MADE: 1962   YEAR OBTAINED: 1967

Doris Borhauer's Notes: This small spruce root basket with lid and rattle in lid was made by Agnes Jacobs in Haines, Alaska, in 1962. Rattle in lid are stones from ptarmigan crop. Purchased at the Craft Shop, Port Chilkoot-Haines, Alaska, May 1967.

>> Mrs. Fannie James

BIOGRAPHY

Mrs. Fannie James was married to George James for sixty-two years, and they lived in Angoon. Her Tlingit name was *Aanshaawátk'i*, reported Harold Jacobs. She was the daughter of Shorty and Anna Johnson. Mr. Johnson had the Tlingit name K̲aachg̲ahéit and was Teikweidí. Mrs. Anna Johnson's Tlingit name was S'eiltín. Mrs. James was a Deisheetaan (Raven-Beaver), from the Raven House, and she was the daughter of Teik̲weidí.

She was born around 1896, and passed away in 1974, when she was seventy-eight years old, said her daughter Selina Everson.

Selina, her only child still alive, said that her mother didn't attend school, though she made sure Selina went to Sheldon Jackson School when she was thirteen years old. Mrs. James had twelve children, and lost six to pneumonia before there was penicillin. Selina remembered, "My mother was a strong lady." Selina grew up with four brothers and one sister. Robert James had five children. Selina has five children, five grandchildren, and five great-grandchildren.

Mrs. Fannie James. *Photo courtesy of Catrina Mitchell and Selina Everson.*

Selina remembers that her mother was very religious, and went to church every Sunday at the Presbyterian Church. "She was active in the missionary, Salvation Army even. . . . " Selina also reports that she was a charter member of Angoon Camp No. 7 of the Alaska Native Sisterhood. Selina said that she loved her Indian dancing and "always made sure we had our regalia." Selina said that her mother brought her children up very strictly. "We were forbidden to go to [dances]." Selina said her mother and father were always putting up food in the summer, and Mrs. James had gardens. "She worked really hard."

Selina reminisced about her mother weaving. "When I would come home from school, I could see her splitting the spruce root[s] and just I would sit and watch her. She would dampen the spruce roots. It just amazed me. . . . She would use cardboard for the inside to keep it firm and for the lid. It still baffles me how she can do the lid that fits it so well, and put the little sand in a little part of the lid. . . . She did beautiful open weave. . . . She would have an apron when she's doing her basket weaving or when she's doing her moccasins or the tops. She was very fussy about not getting any dirt on it, being clean about it."

Selina said that someone had referred to her mother as "a master weaver from the Angoon area." Selina recalled, "My Uncle Sam Johnson's wife told me one time, 'no one can weave like your mother in that open weave.'" Mrs. James worked in the canneries, and Selina said that her mother sold her baskets and other crafts when the steamboats came in.

Selina's father and brothers helped her mother gather spruce roots when her mother was older, Selina recollected. Selina said, "She had . . . the old-fashioned five-gallon coffee cans. She had dye in it. She would lie the spruce root in there until they took the color. I can just see in my mind how she did her roots when she was dying it."

Mrs. James probably learned from her own mother, Selina thought. She did not teach Selina because Selina went away to school, which Selina regrets. "She had talent for art and it passed me by. . . . I feel so sad that I did not sit down and insist on her teaching me." Mrs. James did teach Selina to bead, and she tried to teach Selina's daughter, Donnelle, to weave, but apparently her granddaughter was too young. Selina's daughter, Catrina, has learned to weave Ravenstail later in life, so the weaving tradition continues in the family.

National Park Service Catalog No. 751

YEAR MADE: 1967   YEAR OBTAINED: 1968

Doris Borhauer's Notes: This small spruce root basket with rattle in lid was made by Mrs. George (Fannie) James, November 1967, Angoon, Alaska. The roots for this basket were pulled and prepared for weaving in the fall of 1966. Purchased from Mrs. James, March 1968.

>> Mrs. Mary (John D.) James

BIOGRAPHY

Mrs. Mary James was married to John D. James, who was the uncle of Steve Johnson Sr.'s father, A. P. Johnson. Steve remembered John D. James, and remembered meeting his wife. Steve said that John James was Kiks.ádi, so logically, Mary would have been from the Eagle Moiety, perhaps Chookaneidi or Kaagwaantaan.

Steve remembered her from after World War II, in the 1950s, and said she was at least in her seventies at that point. They lived near the ANB Hall, next to Thompson's store and the old jail. Census records from 1920 record that her first name was Mary, and that she was forty-seven years old at the time, which would put her year of birth around 1873. Her husband, John D. James, was forty-nine years. Also listed were two children, Alice (thirteen years old) and Emma (nine years old), which are probably the girls in the picture to the right. Steve Johnson doesn't remember any children, and none are listed in the 1930 Census.

Mrs. John James and family. *Photo courtesy of Steven Johnson Sr.*

Steve remembered, "She used to tease her husband by calling him Johnnie Jim. He didn't like that."

Steve said that his family had several of her baskets, and he had a berry basket made by her, as well as a lamp. He recalled, "She was a good weaver. We have some of the baskets that she made. Some of them had those little ptarmigan stones [from the bird's crop]. I think I have a berry basket that she made."

Steve knew the minister who sold one of the baskets to Lila Berg, and who was helping Mrs. James, Reverend Elwood Hunter, a Presbyterian minister. Steve said the reverend liked to take a rowboat out and study sea life.

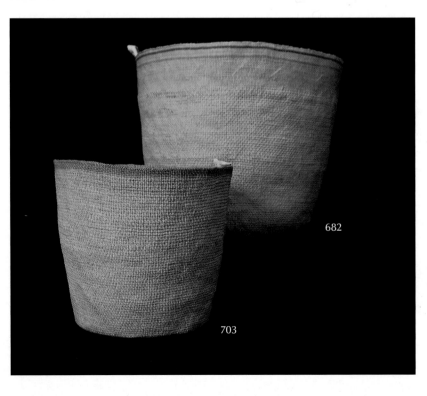

682

703

YEAR MADE: CA. 1900

YEAR OBTAINED: 1949

Doris Borhauer's Notes: This large, plain, spruce root basket with was made by a Sitka Thlingit Indian woman in about 1900 (weaver's name unknown) for utility purposes. The cloth tabs remain on the sides showing it was to be used as a carrying pail for berries, clams, or water. It was purchased from Mrs. John D. James in 1949, through Reverend Elwood Hunter, by Mrs. Lila C. Berg. Mrs. James is the aunt of Charles Benson, still residing in Sitka.

Previous owner: Lila Brougher Berg

YEAR MADE: CA. 1875

YEAR OBTAINED: 1947

Doris Borhauer's Notes: This extra-large spruce root basket with canvas tabs was a carrying basket. It was made by Mrs. John D. James (date unknown), a Thlingit Indian woman. Sitka purchased by Lila Berg in 1947 through the Reverend Elwood Hunter who was helping Mrs. James. These spruce root baskets were made fifty to seventy-five years ago for utility purposes by a Thlingit woman of Sitka, Alaska.

Previous owner: Lila Brougher Berg

Detail of basket No. 682

>> Mrs. Lilly Hoolis John

BIOGRAPHY

Lilly Hoolis John. *Photo courtesy Harold Jacobs.*

Mrs. Lilly Hoolis John was married several times, most notably to Willis Hoolis (Doris Borhauer refers to her as Mrs. Willis Hoolis), and to Mr. John, according to her granddaughter, Anne Johnson, who spent a lot of time with her grandmother. Harold Jacobs noted that Mrs. Lilly Hoolis John was L'eeneidí from the Auke Village in Juneau, and her Tlingit name was *Seikóoni*.

Anne said that her grandmother's sister was Mrs. Katherine Dimitri, who was older than Mrs. Hoolis John. Anne said that her grandmother had another sister, Mrs. Thompson, whose husband had a little store on the waterfront in the Sitka Indian Village, but Anne did not know Mrs. Thompson was her grandmother's sister until after she died. Anne knew her grandmother was born in Juneau and thought her grandmother might have been raised in Sitka or might have come to Sitka when she got married. Jean (Andrews) Boone-Hamar, who wove a basket in this collection, said that Mrs. Hoolis John was her godmother, and remembered her from when Jean was young.

Mrs. Hoolis John was the mother of Anne's father. Anne spent a lot of time with her grandmother, until she was eleven years old and her family moved from Sitka. Anne's family moved back to Sitka, but she didn't see her grandmother as much after that, and her grandmother died when Anne was eighteen or nineteen. Anne learned to speak Tlingit from her grandmother. She is a fluent Tlingit speaker who teaches with the Sitka Native Education Program. Anne said her grandmother was a "very, very busy" woman who gathered native food with her husband and later her brother. Mrs. Hoolis John was involved with Alaska Native Sisterhood and Alaska Native Brotherhood, and spent a lot of time working with them. Anne said she was very outspoken, and that she could have started the women's movement. Anne said her grandmother really believed in education, and that's probably why Anne went to Sheldon Jackson.

Anne Johnson remembered her grandmother did a lot of sewing and beading. Mrs. Hoolis John tried to teach Anne to sew, but it didn't take too well. Mrs. Hoolis John was a gifted sewer. She made Anne's clothes and never used a pattern, but the clothes always fit. Anne remembers her grandmother sewing moccasins in particular, and that she would sell these. Anne would pull a little red wagon downtown to sell the moccasins, as other people remember doing to sell Native crafts.

Anne did remember her grandmother weaving baskets on occasion, but thought that maybe Mrs. Hoolis John and her sister Mrs. Dimitri had woven their baskets earlier in life, because she didn't remember them weaving much. Anne remembered that her grandmother did a lot of work at night, so maybe she wove baskets at night. Anne does remember clearly that her grandmother would gather all her materials for basket weaving. They would go out in a boat together (with her grandma's husband or Anne's brother) to get basket materials. Anne remembers her grandmother drying the spruce roots. Anne did not remember her grandmother selling baskets, and thought she just made them as gifts, but said she must have sold them as well.

Anne thought her grandmother probably learned to weave from her mother, because of Doris Borhauer's notes on the "Relative of Mrs. Hoolis," which said that the materials came from Mrs. Hoolis's mother. So, Mrs. Hoolis John's mother most likely taught her, since she had basket weaving materials. Anne said that Mrs. Hoolis John taught Anne's mother to weave. Anne remembers they often worked together.

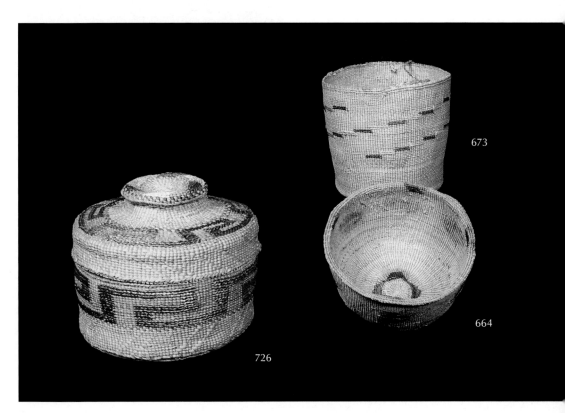

673

664

726

YEAR MADE: 1940   YEAR OBTAINED: 1940

Doris Borhauer's Notes: This dish-shaped spruce basket was made in 1940 by Mrs. Willis Hoolis, a Sitka Thlinget Indian. Purchased by Mrs. L. C. Berg that year. The design is salmonberry.

Previous owner: Lila Brougher Berg

YEAR OBTAINED: 1932

Doris Borhauer's Notes: This spruce root basket, with braided handle, was woven by Mrs. Willis Hoolis, a Sitka Thlingit woman, and presented as a Christmas gift to Lila L. Brougher (village nurse), December 25, 1932.

Previous owner: Lila Brougher Berg

YEAR MADE: CA. 1930
YEAR OBTAINED: 1956

Doris Borhauer's Notes: This covered spruce root basket was made by Mrs. Lilly H. John (former Mrs. Willis Hoolis), a Sitka Thlingit Indian woman, about 1930. It was given to Mrs. E. W. (Nellie) Coulson, sister of Lila Berg, by Mrs. John in 1950. In 1956 it was presented to Lila Berg for her collection.

Previous owner: Lila Brougher Berg

➤➤ Relative of Mrs. Lilly Hoolis John

BIOGRAPHY

Not much is known about the weaver of this basket, because it could not be determined who the relative of Mrs. Hoolis (Lilly Hoolis John) actually was. Mrs. Anne Johnson, granddaughter of Lilly Hoolis John, didn't know who the relative might be, but it was probably a relative on Lilly's mother's side, since it is noted that materials came from Lilly's mother. This relative might have been from the L'eeneidí Clan, since both Mrs. Hoolis John and her mother were L'eeneidí.

YEAR MADE: UNKNOWN
YEAR OBTAINED: 1948

Doris Borhauer's Notes: This small spruce root basket with braided handle was made by a relative of Mrs. Hoolis at Hoonah, Alaska. The pattern is made of grass prepared (dyed) by Mrs. Hoolis's mother many years ago. The basket was presented to Mrs. Lila Berg by Mrs. Willis Hoolis January 7, 1948, as a Russian Christmas gift.

Previous owner: Lila Brougher Berg

➤➤ Mrs. Susie (John) Joseph

BIOGRAPHY

Not much is known about Mrs. Joseph. She was married to John Joseph. Herman Kitka said that she was a close relation of A. P. Johnson's mother, Bessie, who was a Kiks.ádi lady, so Susie Joseph might have been Kiks.ádi.

There was more than one John Joseph in Sitka in the first part of the 1900s. The John Joseph family listed in the 1930 Census, which is closest to when these baskets were made (1931 and 1932), lists John Joseph as sixty-five years old, with a wife Susie, sixty years old and born approximately in 1869. The census also lists a son, George.

Duck Didrickson remembered Mrs. John Joseph, and said, "She was a spry old lady. She walked with her back straight."

685   665

National Park Service Catalog No. 685

YEAR MADE: 1931   YEAR OBTAINED: 1932

Doris Borhauer's Notes: This spruce root basket, with buckle design, was made by Mrs. John Joseph, a Sitka Thlingit Indian, in 1931. Obtained by Miss L. Brougher, R.N., government nurse, from Mrs. Joseph in 1932.

Previous owner: Lila Brougher Berg

National Park Service Catalog No. 665

YEAR MADE: 1932   YEAR OBTAINED: 1932

Doris Borhauer's Notes: This spruce root tray with "waves-of-the-sea" design, on dyed roots, was made by Mrs. John Joseph, a Sitka Thlingit Indian, in 1932, and purchased by Miss L. Brougher, RN, goverment nurse that year.

Previous owner: Lila Brougher Berg

➤➤ Mrs. Katherine "Katy" (Frank) Kitka

BIOGRAPHY

Mrs. Katherine Kitka was married to Frank Kitka. Mrs. Kitka was a Kaagwaantaan, from the Box House, and she came from the Klukwan area originally, according to her son, Herman Kitka Sr., and her daughter, Maria Guthrie. Her husband, Frank, was a leader of the L'uknax.ádi. Mrs. Kitka's Tlingit name was _Kaalagasx_. Mrs. Kitka's maiden name was Bailey. Maria Guthrie said about her parent's marriage: "When

Wedding photo.

she got married to my father, they were both very young, and they never even knew each other. When they got married, they brought them together in the old ways." Mrs. Kitka had at least seven children. One of the baskets was in payment for assistance with the birth of a son, Alexander, but he must have died when he was young.

Maria reported that her mother only went to school until the third grade. Herman said, "They didn't go back then, they just learned their traditional ways." Herman said his mother made "everything else" as well as weaving baskets. Maria remembered, "She spent many hours doing her native arts. She did a lot of moccasin sewing. . . . As a young child, I would sit with her and bead and watch her with her arts." Both Herman and Maria said she also did Chilkat weaving.

Frank and Katherine Kitka, with their children. *Photo courtesy of Mr. Herman Kitka Sr.*

Maria reported that Mrs. Kitka sold her baskets and other crafts to tourists. "We had tour boats that would come in and tie up at the Conway dock. So, as soon as we'd see one coming, we'd all take off and she'd bring out all her things that she had made. Mostly moccasins." Maria said that her mother sold more moccasins than baskets. She said, "A lot of her basketry kind of went out as gifts to special people. I know she sold a few but not too many." Herman said, "You can find her baskets in every collection. She was busy."

Maria reported that her mother mostly wove during the winter, because the family spent summers at fish camp putting up fish and gathering other resources. The family also gathered spruce roots at this time. Maria said, "From what I understand, there is an island not too far away from our campsite where they would go and gather the roots. It had a long sandy beach. When gathering the roots there, it was, the roots were longer, without any knots because as soon as you run into gravel, that's where the root cannot travel, it will turn, and it will develop a knot. So, on the fine sandy beaches is where they gathered these roots." Herman said that he and his dad used to get roots for her. Maria said: "Actually my father was very supportive of her. He helped her with many things, helping her, taking her out to gather her supplies for all her art, native art, that she had done, including the spruce root baskets."

Maria remembered her mother weaving: "In her basketry, she spent hours preparing her materials. She had a very small pocket knife that she used to split and to make sure all her roots were *very* even and straight." Maria recalled one of her mother's baskets in particular. "I know one of her big baskets, I'm not too sure who ended up with it, but she had one great big [basket], it was just huge, I'm sure she brought it, made it for whenever we'd go up to Haines. We still had family ties up there and periodically we'd end going up there and spending time when we were young. And they'd use it to shake soapberries into. Soapberries, you did not handle soapberries with your hands at all, because of the oils from your hands."

Maria talked about her mother being active in the community. Maria said, "She was involved in a lot of different things and she was heavily involved in the ANB/ANS [Alaska Native Brotherhood/ Alaska Native Sisterhood], and she was involved with the Orthodox Church. . . . Outside of all the different kinds of things you were doing for fundraisers for both organizations, it becomes involved." Maria recalled one story about her mother: "Martha Kitka was telling me that at one of the ANB conventions, she had a whole boxful of these baskets that she had made and donated for a fundraiser at Grand Camp one year." Maria remembered attending ANS meetings with her mother, "I can remember going to meetings, and all of it were Tlingit meetings. Our ANB/ANS meetings were in Tlingit. And the place would be full, it would be packed. I can remember sitting on the floor because there was no chair space. All of the older people had elegant speeches. When they talked, there was a lot of protocol."

Maria recalled that she picked up speaking Tlingit from listening to her parents talk to each other, but that the culture was being suppressed in general. "During that time, it's been a sad time for our people to lose so much, because not only did we lose a lot of history, but also we were losing speaking to our parents [at that time]. So what little time I shared with my mother was when I was very young."

Mrs. Kitka learned from her mother how to weave, Herman said. Maria said she learned in Klukwan. Mrs. Kitka taught her older daughter, Liz Walters, how to weave. "[She taught] my sister. My sister sat with her and she wouldn't let me touch the weaving, but she would let my sister. She was older than I [was]. I ended up doing the beading."

Although Mrs. Kitka did not get much schooling, she was skilled in weaving. Her daughter Maria remembers, "It was interesting watching her do some of this basketry. A lot of her designs, I can imagine, were all done in her head, because she couldn't write. And so, it was interesting being able to see how it will go together without following a pattern. Because she had only gone to the third grade, and I'm not sure how much she retained even in counting. I still find it interesting to see the precision and spacing, without the knowledge of counting [in English]." Mrs. Kitka's round basket shows that she was a great designer because it is much harder to make designs on this basket type.

National Park Service Catalog No. 686	National Park Service Catalog No. 709
YEAR MADE: 1931 YEAR OBTAINED: 1931	YEAR MADE: 1931 YEAR OBTAINED: 1931

Doris Borhauer's Notes: This Sitka spruce root basket was made by Mrs. Frank Kitka, a Thlingit Indian woman, in 1931 and presented to Miss Lila Brougher, government nurse, as part payment for a home hygiene textbook.

Previous owner: Lila Brougher Berg

Doris Borhauer's Notes: This spruce root tray, with open work, was made by Mrs. Frank Kitka, a Thlingit Indian, in 1931 for Nurse Lila Brougher who attended her at the delivery of an infant son, Alexander.

Previous owner: Lila Brougher Berg

Detail of bottom of basket No. 709 showing dyed wefts.

>> Mrs. Caroline "Carrie" (George) Lewis

BIOGRAPHY

Mrs. Carrie Lewis was married to George Lewis, a well-known Kiks.ádi leader in the Sitka Tlingit community. She was Da<u>k</u>l'aweidí of the Killerwhale House, from Angoon, although she was raised in Sitka. Her Tlingit name was *Daalnei<u>x</u>'*. Her father was Kiks.ádi. His Tlingit name was *Chanak Éesh*, and her mother's Tlingit name was *<u>K</u>aachkaník*, noted Harold Jacobs. Bertha Karras said that Mrs. Lewis was born in Killisnoo (a former village near Angoon) and came to Sitka to get married.

Bertha Karras was interviewed about Mrs. Lewis. Mrs. Lewis was Bertha's grandmother in the Tlingit way. Mrs. Lewis was the true aunt of Bertha's mother, Mrs. Annie Jacobs. Bertha said she did not have any biological children of her own, but she raised George Lewis Jr. and Ruth Lewis Suckinaw. George Lewis Jr. had four children, Harold W. Lewis Sr., Fredrick M. Lewis Sr., Barbara C. Lewis, and George Dale Lewis, who are grandchildren of Mrs. Lewis. Mrs. Lewis also had a sister who was married to Ralph Young, and they lived near Bertha's family. Mrs. Lewis lived to be eighty-nine years old and died in 1953, soon after her husband.

Mrs. Carrie Lewis, taken from a photo of the 1943 Alaska Native Sisterhood Convention. *Photo courtesy of Harold Jacobs.*

Mrs. Lewis was a schoolteacher, and probably taught at the BIA school in the Sitka Indian Village. Bertha said she spoke very good English, and taught in peoples' homes. She was one of the first Natives to vote, and Bertha talked about how Mrs. Lewis was challenged to know the Constitution before she could vote. "She was one of the first ones that when they voted, they told her she couldn't vote, unless she knew the Constitution of the United States. Then she told them, you say it, then I'll say it. They couldn't say it. So they let her vote."

Bertha remembers, "She was bossy. She would go into any store downtown. If they didn't have a chair, she'd make them bring out a chair to sit down in the store. She was . . . very bold."

Barbara Lewis remembers her grandmother when she lived in Sitka, though she was very young. Her family later moved to Klawock and she did not see her grandmother after that. Barbara said, "I remember we always had to sit quiet [when Grandma wove]. I remember that back then when you go to one of our artist's homes, if they're beading or weaving or knitting or whatever, they used to have a card table set up, and that's where their work is at, and then they'd cover it. You were never, ever, ever to touch it. We always used to wonder what was under there. Then later on I found out the reason they did that was so the work wouldn't get disturbed. They just laid it down where they stopped, and then they'd just pick up where they left off."

Bertha remembered her Grandma, Mrs. Lewis, weaving. "I remember her making baskets. She always had a pan of water and a pan of all these spruce roots soaking. She [was] always a very fine weaver, very fine. She did the finest of any I ever knew. That's real mathematics [in the design]. . . . I could just hear it squeaking when she pulled on the threads [wefts]. There's a name for sounds that she made when she [wove]. She was always—it wasn't humming, it isn't whistling, it's just sss-ssss-sssss. She'd make that sound when she was [weaving]. There's a name for it in Tlingit." Bertha is impressed with how the old weavers did the patterns on their baskets: "My mother said they used rocks to count, to make it come out even. . . . They didn't have any patterns or anything. That's why I think they're so artistic."

Bertha knew that Mrs. Lewis taught others how to weave, and she said she probably taught Bertha's mother. Bertha also weaves baskets, though she did not learn to weave directly from her grandmother or her mother.

"I learned from Delores Churchill. But what's really interesting is that Delores Churchill [a Haida weaver] learned the Tlingit way from my mother [Annie Jacobs]. . . . I used to watch my mother. Then Delores had a different way of weaving, but she taught me the way my mother did. And it wasn't long before I was using my

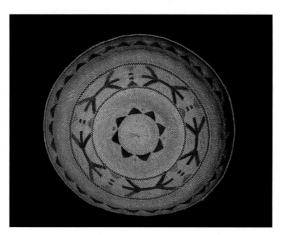

mother's style, without even ever weaving [before]. So I think I must have watched [my mother] enough to use her style of weaving. . . . I could just remember her hands going like this [demonstrates] and my grandma always used that too, that same style."

National Park Service Catalog No. 718

YEAR MADE: 1932   YEAR OBTAINED: 1932

Doris Borhauer's Notes: This spruce root tray was made in 1932 by Carrie Lewis, a Sitka Thlingit Indian, for Mrs. A. L. Brougher, mother of Lila Berg.

Previous owner: A. L. Brougher

▶▶ "Grandma Littlefield" (Mrs. Martha White Littlefield)

BIOGRAPHY

Grandma Littlefield, as she was known, married John Littlefield I, an Englishman in the British Navy who came to Sitka on the well-known ship, the *Jamestown*. No one remembers her directly, but she was the matriarch of the Littlefield family. Grandma Littlefield was of the T'akdeintaan Clan from the Snail House in Hoonah. Her Tlingit name was *Seikóoni*.

The father of Grandma Littlefield was Martin White, who had the Tlingit name *Kuchein*, and was Kaagwaantaan from the Box House. Her mother was only known by her Tlingit name, *Kaastu.ooch*.

Grandma Littlefield had two sons, John and Charlie, and two daughters, Mary and Charlotte Erwin, and has many Littlefield descendents to this day. Her son John Jr. had the Tlingit name *Kashtlin*, and her son Charlie had the Tlingit name *Yoowaak' Eesh*.

Grandma Littlefield was born in 1870, but there is no information about when she died. Her husband died in 1924.

Information on Grandma Littlefield was provided by John Littlefield III, her great-grandson. John's father was Edward, whose father was John Littlefield Jr.

<u>National Park Service Catalog No. 689</u>

YEAR MADE: 1850   YEAR OBTAINED: CA. 1931

Doris Borhauer's Notes: This spruce root basket was made by Grandma Littlefield, a Thlingit Indian woman, whose husband was of the British Navy. She is the mother of John and Charlie Littlefield of Sitka. Basket was made in the year of 1850. The roots are brown with age, not dyed. The background of the pattern are roots dyed with hemlock bark. The white of the pattern is the natural dry grass shade. The red dye is from uric acid of a small boy's urine. This basket was obtained by Lila Brougher, R.N., in about 1931 when she was village nurse at Sitka. Miss Brougher questioned Mrs. Littlefield about the source of the dye for the red color and she timidly and shyly told the secret. This basket was made for ornamental, not utility purposes. The design is "Head of Salmonberry" (*Kla-ol-klink*), "Tree Crotch" (*Kahk-kak-see*), and "Wave" (*Guth-luh-ku*) pattern. Grandma Littlefield was of Raven Clan Hoonah. Her husband, John Henry was born in Hampshire, England. She was grandma to Gregory Littlefield.

Previous owner: Lila Brougher Berg

⟫ Mrs. Miriam Bartlett Littlefield

BIOGRAPHY

Miriam Littlefield was married to Charles "Charlie" Littlefield, son of Grandma Littlefield and John Littlefield I. Mr. Bob Sam said that her maiden name was Bartlett, and her father, George Bartlett, is buried in the Russian Cemetery. However, not much is known about her. She apparently had no children, and died before 1940. Her husband, Charlie, was later married to Ester Kasakan Littlefield, who was well known for her beading and basket weaving. Ester was the mother of Charlie's children, and they do not know much about his first wife.

Harold Jacobs noted that Miriam Bartlett Littlefield was from the Box House of the Kaagwaantaan Clan. Her mother was Susie Marshall, and her father, George Bartlett, had the Tlingit name *Naayi Éesh*, and was Kiks.ádi.

Miriam might have been born in 1902. The 1920 Census lists George Bartlett, his wife Suzy, and his daughters Ruth, Madge, and Annie. Madge might have been Miriam.

BASKETS ON NEXT PAGE.

National Park Service Catalog No. 706

YEAR MADE: 1930   YEAR OBTAINED: 1930

Doris Borhauer's Notes: This spruce root basket, made to hold a whiskbroom, was woven in 1930 by Mrs. Miriam Bartlett Littlefield (Charlie), a young Thlingit Indian woman, at Sitka. Purchased by Lila Brougher in 1930.

Previous owner: Lila Brougher Berg

National Park Service Catalog No. 720

YEAR MADE: 1930

Doris Borhauer's Notes: This spruce root open weave covered basket was made in 1930 by Miriam Bartlett Littlefield (Mrs. Charles) to give in payment for her home hygiene textbook to Lila Brougher, government nurse who conducted home hygiene classes for Indian women of the village, at the Sitka government school.

Previous owner: Lila Brougher Berg

▶▶ Mrs. Mary Marks

BIOGRAPHY

Mary Marks was a well-known weaver in Sitka. She was also known as Grandma Marks. Mrs. Marks was Kiks.ádi. According to Harold Jacobs, Mrs. Marks's Tlingit name was *S'eistaan Tláa*, and she was from the Clay House of the Kiks.ádi. Harold noted that her father was Jimmy Andrews, his Tlingit name was *Jeex'wan Éesh*, and he was Chookaneidí, from the Iron House in Sitka. The mother of Mrs. Marks was Susie Andrews and she had the Tlingit name *Jeextsoow*.

Mrs. Marks was first married to Smarty Jacobs and had one son, Charlie Jacobs. Charlie had one son, George Jacobs, who is a grandson of Mrs. Marks. Mrs. Marks married Frank Marks after her first husband died, and they had three daughters: Liz Hill, Emily Williams, and Selina Wrenn.

Mrs. Marks was close to her granddaughter, Camille Ferguson, who shared information about her. Camille's mother was Selina Wrenn. Emily Williams, Mrs. Marks' daughter, was also interviewed for this project, and passed away shortly after the interview.

Mrs. Marks was in her early seventies when Camille was born, so she was always elderly when Camille knew her. She was one hundred years old when she died, and she was born in 1888 or 1889. Camille said her grandmother did not have a birth certificate, because she was born at fish camp. Mrs. Marks worked in a cannery. She owned an island, known as Marks Island by Cape Barunof, which she used with her husband. They had a garden there, and it was taken by the Army for use in World War II and never returned to her family.

Camille said that her grandmother wove baskets and did other crafts. "Growing up she not only [wove] baskets, but sewed moccasins, hand-sewed clothes, she did everything." Camille recalls her grandmother weaving well. "It was neat to watch her because she almost did it without looking. It was like the knitting. It was fascinating to see. All [of the weaving was] perfect." Camille recalled the elaborateness of her grandmother's work. "Then there were intricate [baskets] around a fancy bottle. They were really, really tiny weaves." Emily Williams, Mrs. Marks's daughter, remembered that her mother and her mother's sister used to weave during the evening, when the weather was getting warmer.

Mary Marks working on moccasins. *Photo from* Sitka Sentinel.

Mrs. Marks mostly wove baskets for income. Camille said, "She said the reason why she learned it and [did it] was for income. You can sell it to the tourists. . . . But everything she did was either for sale to feed her family. [It] was her income. That's why you see her baskets in different places." John Bartels recalls how she had priority for the good spot to set up her table to sell to the tourists. The best spot was in front of Ellis Air, where the planes pulled up, and this is where she would set up.

Mrs. Marks told her granddaughter about getting materials to make baskets. Camille remembered, "I remember asking her, 'Where did you get the roots from?' You got out in the boat, to the special place to get them. We don't always go to the same place to get them. You go out in the boat and find the tree by itself. You go. Every time I see a tree out in a spit area. . . . You get [the roots] as long as you can." Camille said she asked her grandmother what she used to split her roots before razor blades, and her grandmother told her they used a mussel shell. Camille also remembered the different colors used in the decoration: "She used different colors in some of her weaving. I still have them: orange, yellow, brown, and I think there is green." Mrs. Marks used Rit dye when Camille watched her, and Camille asked what she used before Rit dye. Camille recalled that her grandmother told her, "Before [the Native women] would use candy bar wrappers. They were Hershey wrappers. [Grandma] could not use them anymore because they changed the wrappers. I thought that was fascinating because I never would have thought of that." Emily Williams, daughter of Mrs. Marks, remembered that they made a paste from mountain ash tree berries that they used for dye.

Mrs. Marks learned to weave from her great-aunt, according to Emily Williams. Camille said she had a picture of her grandmother's aunt weaving, so weaving has a long run in her family. Mrs. Marks did try to teach Camille how to weave. "My grandma said I should learn on the best: spruce roots. It is a lot easier to learn on spruce

Mary Marks, right, with sisters. *Photo courtesy of Camille Ferguson.*

roots. She was so fast I could not keep up with what she was doing." Camille talked about her difficulties learning to weave: "When I would try, I did not understand, I did not have those nimble fingers that she had." Emily, Mrs. Marks's daughter, also wove. "[Emily] is my aunt. I think she [wove] baskets. She came over to my house and saw two unfinished baskets and wanted to finish them."

Probably Mary Marks, foreground, selling baskets to tourists on Lincoln Street. *Photo courtesy of Camille Ferguson.*

YEAR MADE: 1967   YEAR OBTAINED: 1968

Doris Borhauer's Notes: This spruce root basket with grass overlay design of "one within another" and "labret" was made by Mrs. Mary Marks, Thlingit Indian of Sitka, Alaska, in 1967. Purchased from Mary Marks June 1968.

YEAR MADE: 1967   YEAR OBTAINED: 1967

Doris Borhauer's Notes: This small spruce root basket was made in Sitka, Alaska, by Mrs. Mary Marks in March 1967. Purchased in March 1967 from Mrs. Mary Marks.

YEAR MADE: 1967   YEAR OBTAINED: 1967

Doris Borhauer's Notes: This small spruce root basket was made in Sitka by Mrs. Mary Marks, a Thlingit Indian woman, in February 1967 and purchased on that date from Mrs. Marks.

►► Mrs. Mary Miller

BIOGRAPHY

Not much is known about Mrs. Mary Miller directly. She does have descendents alive today, but because Mrs. Miller lived long ago, they did not know her. Mrs. Mary Miller's daughter was Mary Skeek. Mary Skeek and her mother were originally from Auke Bay and were of the Wooshkeetaan Clan. Mary Skeek went to Kake to marry Paddy Skeek and lived there the rest of her life. After her husband passed, her son, George Skeek, his wife, Helen, and their family moved in with her to help her in her later years. Mary had three sons, who have all passed away.

Mrs. Mary Skeek's daughter-in-law, Helen Skeek, is alive today and is ninety-four years old. She has seven surviving children: Lucy Clewis, Ann Tyone, Wilfred Skeek, Wesley Brown Sr., Wilbur Brown Sr., Matthew Brown Sr., and Edna Charley. Lucy, Ann, and Wilfred are Wooshkeetaan Yadi (children of the Wooshkeetaan Clan) and Wesley, Wilbur, Matthew, and Edna are Tanaadi Yadi (children of the Tanaadi Clan). Mary Skeek was not only a mother and grandmother, but she was also a basket maker, gardener, historian, and midwife. She delivered many, many babies in Kake, including some of her own grandchildren.

Because of her health and age, Helen now lives in Anchorage with Lucille and Tony Clewis.

Mrs. Mary Skeek (seated), daughter of Mary Miller. Pictured with her son, George Skeek, and his wife, Helen Skeek, who sold the baskets to Doris Borhauer. *Photo courtesy of Lucille Clewis.*

Lucy asked her mother about the baskets. Helen Skeek actually sold the baskets, but she does not remember this. Lucy and her mother remembered the baskets that Mary Skeek gave them. "There was one basket my grandma Mary gave to her. They used to use it for berry picking. . . . [My mother] said she had several of them, but she did not know what happened to them."

Mary Skeek had close relationships with her grandchildren. The family has many good memories of her. Because of her petite stature, her grandchildren referred to her as "Small Gramma." Helen Skeek remembers using a basket for berry picking. Wesley Sr. remembers gathering roots for her basket making. Wilbur Sr. remembers learning to Indian dance because of her encouragement. Edna remembers that she talked about her basket and mat making and that visitors often came to hear her stories, legends, and history. Lucy, Ann, and Wilfred have memories of her singing and teaching them to dance at a very young age. Mary Skeek was one of the singers of the Tlingit dancers in Kake at the time. Lucy said, "I remember she used to sing in the dance group. That was when I was about six or seven years old. . . . We had fun, but they were really strict with us, telling us that we were not supposed to smile when we were dancing." Because of "Small Gramma's" influence her grandchildren retained much of their Tlingit values and culture that in turn is being passed on to their children and grandchildren. Mary Skeek died in 1967. She was eighty-four years old.

>> Mother of Mary Miller

BIOGRAPHY

This basket was made by the mother of Mary Miller, who also wove baskets in this collection. See the previous biography on Mary Miller. Even less is known about the mother of Mary Miller than Mary Miller herself. The mother of Mary Miller would have been Wooshkeetaan, as were her daughter, Mary Miller; her granddaughter, Mary Skeek; and her great-grandson, George Skeek. According to the notes, the mother of Mary Miller lived in Juneau, like her daughter. The mother of Mary Miller might have been born in the 1840s. The basket she made is probably one of the oldest in this collection, and it is at least the oldest basket with a definite date when it was made. This is also the only cooking pot, and was actually used to cook seaweed.

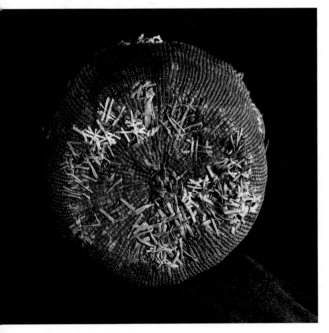

The bottom of this basket (No. 750) shows repairs from its use as a cooking vessel.

National Park Service Catalog No. 750

YEAR MADE: 1867   YEAR OBTAINED: 1968

Doris Borhauer's Notes: This spruce root cooking pot was made by Mrs. Mary Skeek's grandmother in 1867 in Juneau, Alaska. Mrs. Mary Skeek, whose birthdate is September 30, 1883, was living with her son and daughter-in-law, Mr. and Mrs. George Skeek (Helen), in Kake, Alaska, when she passed away December 12, 1967. Seaweed was placed in this pot, then hot rocks were dropped in to cook the seaweed. After Mrs. Mary Skeek returned to Kake from Juneau she used this pot for berry picking. Purchased from Mrs. George (Helen) Skeek. Kake, Alaska, February 1968.

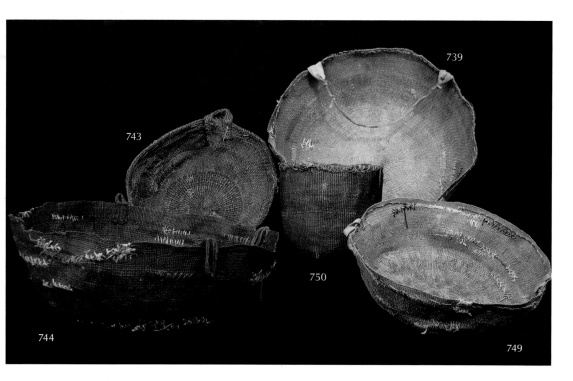

National Park Service Catalog No. 739

YEAR MADE: 1880   YEAR OBTAINED: 1967

Doris Borhauer's Notes: This spruce root berry basket was made by Mrs. Mary Miller, a Thlingit Indian woman in Juneau, Alaska, in 1880. Following Mrs. Miller's death, the basket was acquired by her daughter, Mrs. Mary Skeek. Mrs. Skeek, whose birthdate is September 30, 1883, was married in Kake, Alaska, and resides there now with her son and daughter-in-law, Mr. and Mrs. George Skeek. Purchased from Mrs. Mary Skeek, Kake, Alaska, in May 1967.

National Park Service Catalog No. 743

YEAR MADE: 1908   YEAR OBTAINED: 1967

Doris Borhauer's Notes: This large spruce root berry basket was made in 1908 by Mrs. Mary Miller, a Thlingit Indian woman in Juneau, Alaska. Mrs. Miller gave this basket to her daughter, Mrs. Mary Skeek, whose birth-date is September 30, 1883. Mrs. Mary Skeek was married in Kake, Alaska, and resides there now with her son and daughter-in-law, Mr. and Mrs. George Skeek (Helen). Mary Skeek gave this basket to Helen Skeek who also used it for berry picking. Purchased from Mrs. Helen Skeek, Kake, Alaska, in June 1967.

National Park Service Catalog No. 744

YEAR MADE: 1906   YEAR OBTAINED: 1967

Doris Borhauer's Notes: This large spruce root berry basket with the four tabs was made by Mrs. Mary Miller, a Thlingit Indian woman in Juneau, Alaska, in 1906. Mrs. Miller gave this basket to her daughter, Mrs. Mary Skeek. Mrs. Skeek, whose birthdate is September 30, 1883, was married in Kake, Alaska, and resides there now with her son and daughter-in-law, Mr. and Mrs. George Skeek (Helen). Purchased from Mrs. Helen Skeek, Kake, Alaska, in July 1967.

National Park Service Catalog No. 749

YEAR MADE: 1915   YEAR OBTAINED: 1968

Doris Borhauer's Notes: This spruce berry basket was made by Mary Skeek's mother, Mrs. Anna Miller in Juneau, Alaska, 1915. Mrs. Miller gave this basket to her daughter, Mrs. Mary Skeek, whose birthdate is September 30, 1883. Mary Skeek was married in Kake, Alaska, moved to Juneau, and then returned to Kake to live with her son and daughter-in-law, Mr. and Mrs. George Skeek (Helen), until her death December 12, 1967, at the age of eighty-four. Purchased in February 1968 from Mrs. George (Helen) Skeek.

Note for basket No. 749: Although Doris Borhauer noted Anna Miller made this basket, she is Mary Miller (mother of Mary Skeek), the same person who made the other baskets.

>> Mrs. Mary Paul

BIOGRAPHY

There is some confusion as to whether Mary Paul actually wove this basket. According to her granddaughter, Roberta Wolfe, who talked to her mother, Mary Paul's daughter Gertrude Wolfe, Mary Paul did not weave baskets. Roberta Wolfe wrote, "I talked to my mom and she said that my gram never did weave. The weaver was my namesake *Xaak du kaa*."

Other elders in the Sitka community thought she did weave, but nothing has been confirmed.

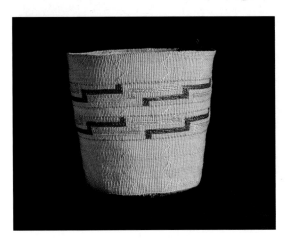

National Park Service Catalog No. 712

YEAR OBTAINED: 1932

Doris Borhauer's Notes: This finely woven spruce root basket was made by Mrs. Frank (Mary) Paul, Sitka Thlingit Indian woman, and offered in payment to the government nurse, Miss Lila Brougher, for her home hygiene textbook in March 1932.

Previous owner: Lila Brougher Berg

>> Mrs. Selina Peratrovich

BIOGRAPHY

Mrs. Selina Peratrovich was a Haida woman, who was born Selina Victoria Harris. Selina is widely known as an excellent basket weaver and teacher, perpetuator of native basket weaving. Her daughter, Delores Churchill, a renowned basket weaver and teacher, talked about her mother. Mrs. Peratrovich was born in Massett, British Columbia, but spent a lot of her childhood years in Howkan, Alaska (where she knew Lydia Charles, another Haida weaver). She grew up living with her grandmother, who moved back to Howkan so Selina could be near her mother, whom Selina missed.

Mrs. Peratrovich had ten children, though several of them died young. All of Selina's extended family died in the flu epidemic right after the First World War: her mother, grandmother, brother, and brother's children. Mrs. Peratrovich had several daughters, Julia, May, Delores, and Jane, who is recognized as the family matriarch.

According to Delores, Selina's grandmother did not teach her many life skills because she wanted to keep Selina from being married off when she was young. Selina did get married at seventeen or eighteen, when her uncles came to take her to get married to Delores's father. Delores said, "She didn't learn [to weave] from her mother or her grandmother because grandmother really didn't want her to be eligible to marry young, so she kept her kind of ignorant. But when she married, her mother-in-law (Delores paternal grandmother) was always weaving baskets. So mother asked her, 'Could you teach me?' And she said, 'No my dear, when you have small children, you have to pay attention to small children. When you start weaving you forget about cleaning house, you forget about taking care of your children, so no, I'm not going to teach you.' But my mother kept sitting around, talking to her. And one day she finished a basket and gave it to my grandmother, my paternal grandmother. And my grandmother was really surprised and started teaching her because she was a good weaver."

Selina taught many people how to weave, especially in her later years. In her earlier years, Delores remembers that her mother taught Isabel Rorick, a famous Haida hat maker, and Florence Davidson, her best friend who also got married quite young, and Selina taught Delores's daughter, April Churchill. "My daughter April learned from my mother. And my mother said the same thing to her. She said to April, you know I'm not going to teach you to weave because you have little kids. But April sat there with her grandmother, watching her, and she learned. And one day she put a basket down, and my mother said, 'Wow, who did that?' And April said, 'I did.' And so my mother started working with her and teaching her. And she would buy all her baskets. She never ever bought mine. [laughter] But she would buy all of April's baskets and give them away to people as gifts. April is really gifted."

Selina also taught her daughter Delores to weave. Selina first taught Delores when she was in school. "My mother came to class to teach basketry. Well everybody—she was making them make cylindrical

Mrs. Selina Peratrovich teaching a girl to weave. *Photo courtesy of Delores Churchill.*

baskets. Everybody would listen to her. She'd say, Take it undone. Do it again. Because they were kind of, you know how baskets either convex or concave when you first start. And I wouldn't listen, I don't know whether mine was convex or concave, but I just kept weaving. . . ." Delores stopped weaving after the first basket, and later in school she was told she wasn't artistic, so she didn't think she could weave baskets.

Later, after Delores's husband encouraged her, Delores took a class at the community college from her mother, who taught her reluctantly. "[Delores told her husband] 'I don't think I could weave, my mother thinks I can't.' [My husband] said, 'well, I think you should sign up at the university class.' Because my mother was teaching at Ketchikan Community College. So I signed up for the class, I was late because I had to work late at the office. . . . I came into the room, and she said in her broken English, 'What you do here? I weave, I weave, you no look. Go on, go home.' I didn't know what to do, because I'd never answered her. I'd always been rebellious, but I never ever spoke back to her. So I stood there not knowing what to do. And then the head of the art department . . . walked into the classroom, and he said, 'What's going on?' I said she said I can't take the class. He said, 'Selina, we need her registration.' So I got to stay and but she made me take it undone over and over and over. My poor basket was in shreds. I finally made it. But by the time the class was over, I was addicted."

Delores remembers her mother worked very hard at weaving. "She really worked on it like a job. . . . I mean, she would get up at like 5:30 in the morning, and she really felt it important that her house be clean before she did anything, because she said if your house was messy and you wove, your weaving would be messy too." Selina had set times when she would weave. "She wove in the morning for like two hours, and then she wove in the afternoon for two hours, and then she wove in the evening for two hours. So they were separate, . . . she never wove all at one time because she said your back got too sore. She always sat really straight when she wove. Like I slump over sometimes when I weave, but not her, she always sat perfectly, kept her back really straight. So her back was always straight even in her old age because of that."

Selina was one of the most prolific teachers in Alaska, and taught many people, Tlingit, Haida, and otherwise, how to weave baskets. Delores said she did this because she was afraid of the art dying out. "I think what I really admired about her was that she really was dedicated in perpetuating the art. She was really scared when I read [a] letter to her [from a collector who said basket weaving was a dying art], she took it really seriously and decided she was going to [teach]. She didn't say it to me, but in her actions from then on, she was teaching wherever anyone wanted her. Yakutat, Craig, Bethel . . . I mean . . . I think she really got people interested in their own basketry, like in the Bethel area. I really think she was instrumental in not saying anything, but just doing it, and showing people it was important. I think she really was very instrumental in keeping this basketry art going. . . . When I look back and think about her teaching twenty and thirty people at the state museum, people just standing around her, watching her and getting interested, I think she had a lot to do with that. Because people were calling her, not just Haidas, but Tlingits and Tsimshians, saying . . . we don't teach other people, we only teach our families, we only teach our nephews and nieces, we don't teach other people. And she got threats. She didn't listen. She just kept right on doing it, because people were saying you shouldn't be teaching it, because it's intellectual property that belongs in the clan. So she had a lot to put up with. Yah, it was really incredible, the pressure that she got from everyone. But she kept right on, because to her it was really, really important that this art form not be lost. Whether she said it verbally or not, she did it with her life, showing how important it was. And she was really stunning."

National Park Service Catalog No. 740

YEAR MADE: 1964   YEAR OBTAINED: 1967

Doris Borhauer's Notes: This small spruce root basket with lid was made by Mrs. Salina Peratrovich, a Tsimshian [sic] Indian woman in Ketchikan, in 1964. Purchased from Mrs. Mona Jackson, neice of Salina Peratrovich, in Kake, Alaska, in May 1967. [Mrs. Peratrovich is actually Haida.]

➤➤ Mrs. Lottie Peters

BIOGRAPHY

Mrs. Lottie Peters was married to William Peters. Ida Peters, Mrs. Peters' daughter-in-law, thought that Mrs. Peters was from the Kaagwaantaan Clan (Eagle-wolf). According to Harold Jacobs, her Tlingit name was Kaax̲k'wei. Her granddaughter, Andréa Craig, daughter of Ida Peters, said that Mrs. Peters's maiden name was Plotnikoff, and that Mrs. Peters father was half Russian. Harold Jacobs gave further detail, noting that her father was Yakov Plotnikoff, also known as Jacob Carpenter (the translation from Russian), and that her father was Koosk'eidí from the Cow House, and his Tlingit name was Koon Éesh. Mrs. Peters mother was Natalia, and her Tlingit name was K̲uwteen, and they were both from the Box House of the Kaagwaantaan.

According to a newspaper clipping from the time of Mrs. Peters' death, Mrs. Peters spent her whole life in Sitka. She was born in 1880. Mrs. Peters had eleven children. The obituary of Mrs. Peters listed her children alive at the time of her death as Annie Littlefield, Matilda Monzon, Flora Gamble, Andrew Peters and Andréa's father, Bill Peters (William Peters Jr.). Bill married Andréa's mother, Ida Peters. The newspaper article also noted that Mrs. Peters was Russian Orthodox and was a member of St. Michael's Cathedral, and she was also a member of the Alaska Native Sisterhood.

Andréa did not know that her grandmother ever wove baskets, but Andréa's mother, Ida did remember her weaving. Ida Peters, Mrs. Peters' daughter-in-law, said that Mrs. Peters learned from her mother. Ida remembers that her mother-in-law went out and harvested spruce roots and other basket making materials.

Andréa spent some time with her grandmother, Mrs. Peters, because "She took care of us [children] while my mother was at work." Andréa said that her grandfather, William, had died in 1942, before she was born. Andréa said that her grandmother spoke mostly in Tlingit. Her grandmother lived in the same house in the Indian Village with Andréa's family, until it burned down around 1945, and they lost everything. After that, Andréa thought that her grandmother lived with her Auntie Annie (Littlefield). Andréa said that her grandmother died in 1955, and, that she was seventy-five years old when she died.

Lottie and William Peters Sr. *Photo from Ida Peters given to SNHP.*

Mrs. Peters was a gifted weaver, who did very fine work. There is a charming story in the notes for basket 719 about Mrs. Peters "giving" the basket to Lila Berg. This large basket is a wastepaper basket. The other basket is a finely woven flower vase, which still has a twig in the bottom from being used.

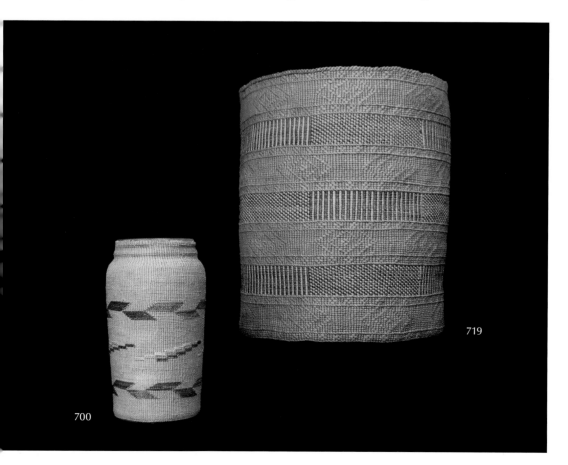

719

700

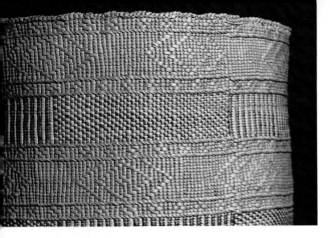

Detail of basket No. 719

Detail of basket No. 719

National Park Service Catalog No. 700
YEAR MADE: CA. 1932

Doris Borhauer's Notes: This spruce root basket, woven over a mayonnaise jar for a vase, was made by Mrs. William (Lottie) Peters Sr., a Sitka Thlingit woman, for Miss Lila Brougher while she was village nurse, about 1932. The pattern is of fireweed blossoms and wild geese flying. Native dye was used.

Previous owner: Lila Brougher Berg

National Park Service Catalog No. 719
YEAR MADE: 1933   YEAR OBTAINED: 1933

Doris Borhauer's Notes: This spruce root wastebasket (for papers or magazines) was made by Mrs. William (Lottie) Peters Sr. in the spring of 1933. She was a Thlingit Indian woman. Mrs. Peters presented it to their government nurse, Lila Brougher, on the event of her marriage, with the following statement, "This basket used to sell for $25.00, now only $15.00. It only cost you $10.00. I give you wedding present on it!" It was sold. The roots of this basket were dyed brown with hemlock bark before weaving. The pattern is made of roots dyed with blueberry juice.

Previous owner: Lila Brougher Berg

Note for basket No. 719: This is a particularly beautiful basket to weavers. Besides its evenness of form, the designs are simple yet incorporate techniques used in Northwest Geometric (Raven's tail) weaving (shown in detail: Basket 719-06). The colored patterns alternate between simple "cockleshell" and "strawberry patch." Mrs. Peters also used skip-stitch, a technique with the weft, to create beautiful designs between the colored sections (shown in detail).

➤➤ Mrs. Isabelle Sam

BIOGRAPHY

Mrs. Isabelle Sam was married to John Sam, of the T'akdeintaan Clan. She was from the Kaagwaantaan Box House, and she came from the Bailey family. Mrs. Sam was a sister to Herman Kitka's mother, Mrs. Frank Kitka, another weaver in this collection. Mrs. Sam had two Tlingit names, one was *L.átk'* according to Harold Jacobs, and the other one was *Seikóoni* according to her grandson, Robert (Bob) Sam, who said it was a name of distinction.

Mrs. Sam had six children: Martha Blankenship and Allen, Frank, Henry, Jake, and John Sam. Allen died young. Mrs. Sam raised her grandson Bob Sam, who was the son of Jake Sam. Bob also has nine siblings, so Mrs. Sam had many descendents. Mrs. Sam also helped to raise Oscar Bennett as a foster son.

Bob said that although Doris Borhauer's notes indicate that a weaver named Mary Sam wove this basket, it was really his grandmother who wove the basket. His grandfather, John Sam, was indeed married to a Mary before his grandmother, but she died young, before the baskets in this collection were made.

Bob said that his grandmother was a midwife. Mrs. Sam was Russian Orthodox and her church name was Sophia. Mrs. Sam could speak English but chose to speak Tlingit exclusively in her later years, which made it difficult for Bob to communicate with her. Bob said she did this because she loved her culture so much. "I dream about my grandmother a lot, and oftentimes she's speaking Tlingit, and she [did] that a lot when I was small. . . . " Bob said she died in 1976.

Bob remembers his grandmother weaving. "I remember her weaving quite well. . . . She had her own room in the house, and that's where she kept all her weaving materials, sewing materials. Oftentimes, she would take like a small oatmeal box and use it as a container . . . that she would form the baskets around. She'd always recycle everything. Everything that she had, she'd always recycle every part, basketry part, or anything. She'd always recycle."

Bob remembered about her weaving that she liked to use black for false embroidery, and she liked to use the "shaman's hat" design quite often.* She mostly sold her baskets to tourists. Bob helped his grandmother collect

Mrs. Isabelle Sam and husband. *Photo courtesy of Bob Sam.*

her basket making materials. "I used to help her collect materials as a gift as she got older. I was one of her favorite grandchildren. And one of my favorite activities was to help gather materials, like elderberry, and I remember helping to gather grasses off of the beach."

Bob Sam remembers that his grandmother had a group of friends she wove with in the 1950s and 1960s. "Once a week she would have like a lunch with all of her elderly friends. Mary Marks and others would come down to her house and they'd pull out all of the native foods, and they'd have like a potluck. They'd talk about weaving and all kinds of stuff, like elderly ladies do when they get together. It was one of my favorite times."

Bob said she made things to sell to the tourists. She wove baskets, but mostly made dolls and fur purses to sell. "She was one of the elderly ladies that went down town all the time to sell baskets and stuff. A lot of the time she used to go down there with Mary Marks, Mrs. Dimitri, Mrs. Pete Kitka, and another elderly lady named Mrs. Aragon. They all used to sit together in front of Sitka Hotel. There was mostly basketry and moccasins, and little dolls."

Bob said that she sold her baskets for ten or twelve dollars, maybe as much as twenty. Bob remembers helping to go set up to sell to the tourists. "My job as a kid was to take a little red wagon full of baskets and dolls, all the stuff, to take it downtown to be sold, by the Sitka Hotel. I would take my grandmother's wagon down there first, and set it all up and get it ready for her to come down. Then I'd run down and get Mrs. Dimitri's. And then I'd also get Mrs. Aragon's wagon. I really enjoyed doing that, because they paid me fifty cents for doing that. [Bob chuckled] That was a lot of money! So by the end of the day I had about two or three dollars."

*Both baskets in the collection feature the "shaman's hat" pattern.

BASKETS ON NEXT PAGE.

734

737

National Park Service Catalog No. 734	National Park Service Catalog No. 737
YEAR OBTAINED: 1966	YEAR MADE: 1966 YEAR OBTAINED: 1967

Doris Borhauer's Notes: This spruce root open basket was made by Mrs. Mary (John) Sam, a Thlingit Indian woman of Sitka. The native dye was used for the grass design. Purchased from Mrs. Sam by Lila Berg in August 1966.

Previous Owner: Lila Brougher Berg

Doris Borhauer's Notes: This small spruce root basket with handle was made in Sitka by Mrs. Mary (John) Sam, a Thlingit Indian woman, 1966. Purchased in March 1967 from Mrs. Sam.

➤➤ Mrs. Sally Stuteen

BIOGRAPHY

Mrs. Sally Stuteen was the mother of David Stuteen (who was married to Alice Stuteen) and Louise Johnson. Vesta Dominicks, an elder in Sitka, is also related indirectly to Sally Stuteen. Her mother was Alice Stuteen, and her stepfather was David Stuteen, Mrs. Stuteen's son.

Katie Davis was interviewed for this project. Katie is the granddaughter of Louise Johnson, Mrs. Stuteen's daughter. Louise was actually her grandmother's sister or cousin, but these are the same as grandmother in Tlingit culture. Louise was married most notably to Frank Johnson. At the time this basket was sold, though, Louise was married to John Kawsunk. Katie said that Louise had no children of her own. Doris Borhauer noted that Louise Johnson was born in 1888.

Louise was the same clan as Katie, Sitgweidí or S'eet'ḵweidí, which means that Louise's mother Mrs. Stuteen would have been the same clan. The name for the clan means "around glaciers." Topsy Johnson, whose uncle is Frank Johnson, said that Louise's (and Mrs. Stuteen's) clan was from Hookum Bay, near Sumdum. Sumdum is an area south of Juneau that used to be a large ḵwáan or village area, but is now not populated, because all of the people moved to the areas of Juneau, Kake, or Angoon.

YEAR MADE: CA. 1912   YEAR OBTAINED: 1967

Doris Borhauer's Notes: This spruce root bowl-shaped basket is called *Kuh-dutsa-yate* in Thlingit. The name signifies its primary use. In picking blueberries and red huckleberries, they are picked by taking the branches in one hand and holding them over the basket, knocking the berries into the basket. Berries are then put in another container and cleaned later. These baskets are often two feet in diameter.

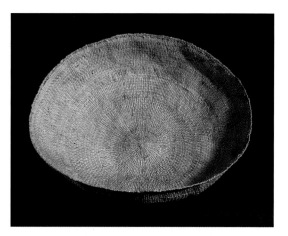

The spruce roots are dug in the spring when the sap starts running. Roots must be straight and free from defects that would make it difficult to split. Roots are heated over a fire and stripped of the covering by pulling each root through a slit in a piece of wood, loosely tied with no sharp bends, to be worked on later. In ancient times, baskets were made waterproof for carrying water and boiling food, as well as for containers for general use. Baskets were woven of coarser splitting for ordinary use. This basket was made by Sally Stuteen and given to her daughter Louise at the time of her marriage to John Kawsunk about fifty-five years ago, 1912. Louise attended Chemawa School in Oregon for about seven years, then returned to Kake, Alaska, to be married. John Kawsunk drowned while fishing. Louise later married Frank Johnson who was a member of the legislature. Louise Johnson was born in Kake, Alaska, on September 25, 1888. Purchased from Louise Johnson in October 1967.

▶▶ Mrs. Tlkenatla— likely Mrs. Mary Tlantech

BIOGRAPHY

It is likely that Mrs. Tlkenatla was Mary Tlantech (also Thlentech and Thlenteach, and pronounced Tlaanteech), who is married to Mike Tlantech in the 1920 census. At the time of that census, Mary was sixty-one, and she was likely born in 1859. Mrs. Mary Tlantech was a basket weaver. She was known for saving the Sitka Indian Village, according to Mr. Bob Sam.

In the Alaska State Digital Archives, it notes that the back of the photo had this written: "Friend of the Whites, also saved them from a massacre by the Indians. Was given a pension by the [Territory] of Alaska in 1920?" Another photo that has a much younger Mary Tlantech with Indian policeman Annahootz and others has accompanying text saying, "In the foreground is Annahootz and beside him is Mary Klan Tech

Mary Thlantuch? Tranvers. *Photo by unknown photographer: Alaska State Library/Alaska State Library Place File/Sitka-Indians-16*

51

[sic], daughter of a subchief of the Kokwanton [sic] Clan. Mary was sent by Annahootz to warn the white population of Sitka on the night of February 6th. . . ."

Bob Sam confirmed this story that in 1878 or 1879, the Indian village was going to attack the white community of Sitka. This was in relation to the events where the U.S. Navy bombarded Angoon and Kake. Bob said, "Mary Tlantech warned the community of that attack and actually . . . stopped the battle from even happening. . . . There was a [Sitka] whaling ship in Angoon that some guy from Kake died [on]. The [Indians] wanted to retaliate. It was a misunderstanding. They wanted something in return for the life that was lost, like blankets or something, money or something. They never acknowledged that so . . . Sitka was going to go to war with the community. And they tore up the Russian Orthodox Native Church and made that into like a fort site, and destroyed it. . . . [Mary Tlantech] actually talked to the clan leaders, [Annahootz], that it would be best not to do. . . . It was the Kaagwaantaans that wanted to go to war. [Annahootz] stepped

Indian Police Force, Sitka 1881
Photo: Alaska State Library/Early Prints of Alaska /297-098

in and prevented it from happening." Bob confirmed that Mary Tlantech was given a pension for the rest of her life from the Territory of Alaska for her help.

She was related to the A. P. Johnson family—A. P. Johnson was originally known as Andrew Peter Tlantech. The Johnson family has descendents today, including Steve Johnson Sr., Steve Johnson Jr., and Edith Johnson.

Detail of design near rim of basket.

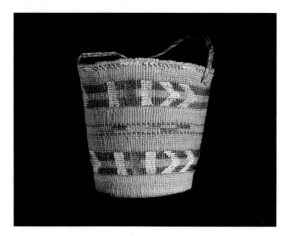

National Park Service Catalog No. 696

YEAR MADE: 1933   YEAR OBTAINED: 1933

Doris Borhauer's Notes: This spruce root basket, with braided handle, was made by Mrs. Tlkenatla, a Sitka Thlingit Indian woman, in 1933 and purchased that year by Miss L. L. Brougher, government nurse. Native dyes were used in this unusual pattern.

Previous owner: Lila Brougher Berg

>> Mrs. Agnes Williams/Agnes Yeltatzie

BIOGRAPHY

Although Doris Borhauer noted that Agnes Williams wove this basket, Delores Churchill, a well-known Haida basket weaver and teacher, thought that Agnes Yeltatzie, also a Haida lady from Massett, wove it. The basket was purchased in the same town (Kake) and year as a basket made by another Haida lady from Massett, Mrs. Lucy Frank. Mrs. Frank's daughter, Mona Jackson, was present when her mother came to Kake and sold her mother's basket. Mona also thought it was woven by Agnes Yeltatzie. It seems likely that Mrs. Frank brought her friend's basket with her to Kake to sell.

Mrs. Yeltatzie has a daughter who is alive, Mary Swanson. Mrs. Yeltatzie was a basket weaver, and her daughter, Mary, said that her logo was a star on top of her basket. Mary said, "She had a star on top. That was her logo for her hats and stuff. She called it a star, it has four points on it." Mary remembers her mother weaving: "My mother used to weave. I used to help her when I was little, I used to do the plaiting for her."

Mrs. Yeltatzie's maiden name was Edenshaw, and her father was Charles Edenshaw, a Haida chief. Mrs. Yeltatzie's clan was Yelgwanaa, Raven Shark House. Mrs. Yeltatzie's husband's father, George, was chief in Howkan, and he was actually half Tlingit. Yeltatzie comes from a Tlingit word. Most of Mrs. Yeltatzie's children were born in Howkan, Alaska, except for Mary and a sister and a brother, who were born in Canada. Mrs. Yeltatzie had twelve children: Ernie, Raymond, Frederick, Charles, Clarence, Lloyd, Willard, Carrie, Clara, Olive, Norma, and Mary. Mary and her sister Norma Adams are the only two children left alive, and they both weave. Yeltatzie grandchildren still living, however.

Mrs. Yeltatzie learned to weave from her mother, Isabelle Edenshaw. Her father and mother, Charles and Isabelle, taught weaving in Sitka. They had Mrs. Edenshaw's baskets, but they burned up when Mrs. Yeltatzie had a house fire. Mrs. Yeltatzie taught all her daughters to weave. "Now all my daughters are learning to weave, they all know how to weave. My youngest, Goldie, is weaving hats right now."

Mrs. Yeltatzie was a hard worker. Mary said of her mother, "She did a lot of weaving. And she used a lot of stuff for her weaving to make colors, different colors to add on to her baskets or hat, whatever she was making. The women here, before we got vehicles, they used to get up at 3 or 4 in the morning, and they'd walk to what we call the North Beach. A whole group of them . . . they'd have their lunches ready and everything. Then they'd start pulling the roots from the ground. They'd stay there the whole day. They'd make the big bonfire, and they burn their roots in the fire. They'd have little boards. They used to put a hole on top and they'd pull the roots through that. . . . A lot of work put into that. The sons that went with them cut a hole in them."

Mary said her mother used to work with cedar bark and spruce root when she wove baskets. They called the grass "wheat" in Haida. She dyed the grass different colors from natural materials. They used alder bark for a reddish color, soil and berries for black, and white shells for white, pounded until they were powder.

Mrs. Yeltatzie spoke both English and Haida, but she only spoke Haida to her children, so her children were fluent speakers. Mary has taught Haida to children in the schools. Mrs. Yeltatzie went to St. Joan's Anglican. Mary remembered they had to go to church every Sunday, and the women had to wear hats. Mrs. Yeltatzie was part of the Women's Auxillary, known as the WA. Mrs. Yeltatzie was raised traditionally, and didn't go to school. There was no electricity or running water when Mrs. Yeltatzie was a child, and they wove baskets and told stories at night.

Mary remembered her mother, "She was so kind. My mother was really easygoing. She never, ever raised her voice. When we did something wrong, she just make us sit down, and she'd tell us it was wrong. [I] never heard her yell, not one time with all the children she had. She was a really gentle person."

Note on Agnes Williams:

There was a woman named Agnes Williams, but little is known about her, and it seems likely she was confused with Agnes Yeltatzie as the maker of this basket. Mrs. Williams was a weaver from Massett. Delores

Churchill, a Haida weaver and daughter of Selina Peratrovich, a weaver of a basket in this collection, thought she remembered Mrs. Williams. Delores said that Mrs. Williams had no relatives after tuberculosis swept through her family. Delores believed that Mrs. Williams husband was *Steeshla* (a Haida name), who was a carver that was from the Eagle Clan, which would make Mrs. Williams a Raven. Delores thought that Mrs. Williams was the aunt to Robert Davidson, a carver in Vancouver, British Columbia. Delores believes that Mrs. Williams was related to Robert Davidson's grandfather's brother, whose last name was Williams. According to Delores, Davidson's grandfather was given a different last name than his brother when they were baptized.

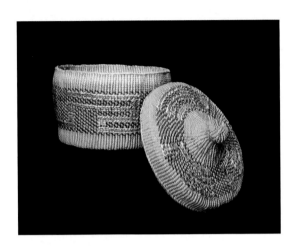

National Park Service Catalog No. 732

YEAR MADE: 1962   YEAR OBTAINED: 1964

Doris Borhauer's Notes: This spruce root basket with a cover was made by Agnes Williams, a Haida Indian of Massett, British Columbia, in 1962. The grass pattern woven on root seed-stitch makes a different design. Purchased at Kake, Alaska, by Mrs. L. C. Berg in 1964.

Previous owner: Lila Brougher Berg

➤➤ Mrs. Sarah (Charlie) Williams

BIOGRAPHY

Mrs. Anne (Emma) Williams Farquhar, the granddaughter of Mrs. Charlie Williams, was interviewed for this project. Earl Williams Sr. and Selina Williams Claggett also talked about their family. Mrs. Farquhar knew her grandmother wove baskets, but Mrs. Farquhar's brother and sister did not remember Mrs. Williams well. Mrs. Farquhar doesn't remember very much about her because their grandmother died when they were all young. Earl barely remembers going to her house. Earl said that her house is still being used, and is up the hill from ANB Hall. Earl said he was less than ten years old when his grandmother died, so she probably died in the 1940s.

Mrs. Charlie Williams was the mother of Cyrus Williams and Peter "Shorty" Williams, according to Earl and Selina. Earl said their father, Cyrus Williams, was Chookaneidí, which would make Mrs. Charlie Williams also from the Chookaneidí Clan, she might have been from the Box House. Earl and Selina also thought that their father's family might have come from near Angoon. Harold Jacobs noted that Mrs. Charlie Williams's Tlingit name was *Kaachkaník*, and she was from the Iron House.

The 1910 Census lists the Charlie Williams family. His wife, Sarah, was born around 1863, and was forty-seven years old at the time of the census. Sarah had nine children, and four of them were living at the time of the census. The children living with her were a son, Peter (nineteen years old, probably Peter "Shorty" Williams), and daughter, Thelma (seven years old). Also listed in the 1910 Census as pupils at Sheldon Jackson School from Sitka are Charles Williams (twelve years old) and Cyrus Williams (thirteen years old, and very likely Sarah and Charlie's son). The same Cyrus Williams is listed in the 1920 Census with his wife, Mary, and infant daughter, Flora, and these are most definitely the parents of Anne, Earl, and Selina. The infant Flora was probably one of the girls for whom the baskets were made.

Mrs. Charlie Williams wove the baskets as berry baskets for her granddaughters, and Mrs. Farquhar was one of the granddaughters, Annie Williams. The mother of Mrs. Farquhar sold the baskets, and

Mrs. Farquhar said her mother used the girls' names on the baskets, Anne and her sisters Selina and Flora. Mrs. Farquhar had two sisters named Selina, and basket No. 675 was woven for the elder sister. Both the first Selina and Flora (Flora Williams Morris) have passed away now. (Selina Claggett, the second Selina, is still alive.)

Baskets:

The three baskets form a set of berry-picking baskets, made for three granddaughters of the same family. Mrs. Mary (Cyrus) Williams, the mother of the girls, sold the baskets apparently when the girls were older. They are all about the same size.

National Park Service Catalog No. 662

YEAR MADE: 1934   YEAR OBTAINED: 1959

Doris Borhauer's Notes: This spruce root basket, with "worm-tread" pattern was made in 1934 by Mrs. Charlie Williams of Sitka, Alaska, for a granddaughter, Annie Williams, when she was small. Purchased in 1959 from Mrs. Cyrus Williams, Annie's mother, by Mrs. L. C. Berg.

Previous Owner: Lila Brougher Berg

National Park Service Catalog No. 675

YEAR MADE: 1934   YEAR OBTAINED: 1959

Doris Borhauer's Notes: This spruce root basket, with tab handles, was made for Selina Williams Hamna to use as a blueberry pail, by her grandmother, Mrs. Charlie Williams, in 1934 when Selina was a child. It was sold to Lila Berg by Selina's mother, Mrs. Cyrus Williams in March 1959. The red seed-stitch of the pattern are dyed spruce roots. (Sitka)

Previous Owner: Lila Brougher Berg

National Park Service Catalog No. 701

YEAR MADE: CA. 1934 YEAR OBTAINED: 1959

Doris Borhauer's Notes: This spruce root basket was made to be used as a blueberry pail. Woven by Mrs. Charlie Williams, a Thlingit Indian woman, for her granddaughter, Flora Williams Morris, when Flora was young, about 1934. Purchased from Flora's mother, Mrs. Cyrus (Mary) Williams, in March 1959 by Lila Berg. Native dye was used in the salmonberry design and also the seed-stitch at the top.

Previous Owner: Lila Brougher Berg

➤➤ Baskets by Unknown Sitka Weavers

The majority of baskets in this collection were woven by Sitka basket weavers. The art of spruce root basketry was especially refined in Sitka, where there was great access to the tourist trade from the steamships that came to visit. Jessie Johnnie noted that there was a basket weaver in every house, and weaving was much more common than now. Basket weaving was one of the few things that brought in some extra money. The weavers in Sitka were especially talented, according to Irene Jimmy. The work of the Sitka basket weavers was very fine, better than the work of contemporary weavers, Irene believes.

Although the weavers who wove the following baskets are not identified, the baskets are wonderful examples of weaving from the Sitka area.

National Park Service Catalog No. 667
YEAR MADE: CA. 1900

Doris Borhauer's Notes: This bowl-shaped spruce root basket was made by a Thlingit Indian woman (name unknown) of Sitka about 1900 (or earlier) and probably used as a bowl for berries. Where the braided handle was is in evidence.

National Park Service Catalog No. 668
YEAR MADE: 1932

Doris Borhauer's Notes: This small spruce root basket—a pin tray—was made in 1932 by a Sitka Thlingit Indian woman (name of weaver unknown). The design on the inside of the basket is a blanket pattern.

National Park Service Catalog No. 672
YEAR OBTAINED: 1932

Doris Borhauer's Notes: This nice spruce root basket was made by a Sitka Thlingit woman (name unknown) and taken in part payment for a home hygiene textbook in 1932 by the village nurse Lila Brougher.

Previous owner: Lila Brougher Berg

National Park Service Catalog No. 674
YEAR MADE: 1930

Doris Borhauer's Notes: This spruce root basket was made in 1930 by a Sitka Thlingit Indian woman (name unknown). The design is "waves-of-the-sea," in plain and dyed grass, on a background of spruce root dyed with hemlock bark.

National Park Service Catalog No. 679
YEAR MADE: CA. 1870
YEAR OBTAINED: 1942

Doris Borhauer's Notes: This old spruce root cup was probably made one hundred years ago in Sitka by a Thlingit Indian woman. It was found in 1942 by the government nurse, Miss Christine Sorrill, in an old house in the village at Sitka. Obtained by Lila Berg for her collection.

Previous owner: Lila Brougher Berg

National Park Service Catalog No. 681
YEAR MADE: 1940   YEAR OBTAINED: 1940

Doris Borhauer's Notes: This small spruce root basket was made in Sitka by a Thlingit Indian woman in 1940. Purchased that year by Lila Berg.

Previous owner: Lila Brougher Berg

National Park Service Catalog No. 683
YEAR MADE: CA. 1900   YEAR OBTAINED: 1935

Doris Borhauer's Notes: This old spruce root carrying pail was found in the Sitka Village in 1935 by Miss Christine Sorrel, R.N., government nurse, and later obtained for Mrs. L. C. Berg's' collection of baskets. Probably it was made about 1900 and has much evidence of use.

Previous owner: Lila Brougher Berg

National Park Service Catalog No. 684
YEAR MADE: 1917

Doris Borhauer's Notes: This spruce root basket was made in 1917 by a Sitka Thlingit Indian woman (name unknown). In 1947 it was obtained from the fine basket collection of Mrs. W. P. Mills by Lila Berg. These baskets were made of spruce roots by Thlingit Indian women of Sitka. The patterns are made with dyed grass and maidenhair for stem. Mr. and Mrs. W. P. Mills left Sitka about 1935. She passed away in 1965. Mr. Mills was responsible for the first water system and for the first electricity in Sitka. A son resides in California.

Previous owner: Mrs. W. P. Mills, Lila Berg

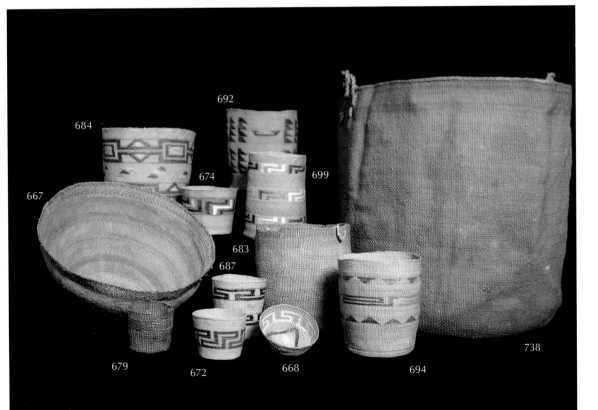

YEAR OBTAINED: 1940

Doris Borhauer's Notes: This spruce root basket was made in Sitka by a Thlingit Indian woman (name unknown). Purchased in 1940 by Lila Berg.

Previous owner: Lila Brougher Berg

YEAR MADE: 1932   YEAR OBTAINED: 1932

Doris Borhauer's Notes: This spruce root basket, with handle, was made by a Thlingit Indian woman (name unknown) at Sitka, Alaska, in 1932. Purchased by L. L. Berg, R.N., that year.

Previous owner: Lila Brougher Berg

YEAR OBTAINED: 1947

Doris Borhauer's Notes: This spruce root basket was made by a Sitka Thlingit Indian woman (date and weaver unknown). Obtained from Mrs. W. P. Mill's collection of fine spruce root baskets in 1947 by Lila Berg.

Previous owner: Mrs. W. P. Mills, Lila Berg

YEAR MADE: CA. 1900

Doris Borhauer's Notes: This old spruce root basket was made by a Sitka Thlingit Indian woman about 1900. Roots are brown with age, not dyed. The hole in one side was made by ink leaking from a fountain pen. The original purchase owner was Mrs. Goddard (rex), then Mrs. O. R. Rutherford, then Mrs. L. C. Berg.

Previous owner: Mrs. Goddard,
Mrs. O. R. Rutherford, Lila Berg

YEAR MADE: 1925   YEAR OBTAINED: 1933

Doris Borhauer's Notes: This spruce root basket was made by a Sitka Thlingit Indian woman in 1925. (name unknown.) Purchased by L. L. B. in 1933.

Previous owner: Lila Brougher Berg

YEAR MADE: CA. 1930 YEAR OBTAINED: 1932

Doris Borhauer's Notes: This spruce root basket was made by a Sitka Thlingit woman about 1930. The grass of the pattern is native dye. Purchased by Lila Berg in 1932.

Previous owner: Lila Brougher Berg

YEAR MADE: 1932

Doris Borhauer's Notes: This spruce root basket, woven to hold a vase for flowers, was made in 1932, by a Sitka Thlingit Indian woman (name unknown). It was sent as a gift to Mrs. Berg's mother, Mrs. A. L. Brougher of Scotts Mills, Oregon. Upon Mrs. Brougher's decease the basket was returned to Mrs. Berg for her basket collection.

Previous owner: Lila Brougher Berg

YEAR MADE: CA. 1920 YEAR OBTAINED: 1935

Doris Borhauer's Notes: This spruce root basket was made by a Thlingit Indian woman in southeast Alaska, perhaps Sitka, about 1920. Weaver unknown. There is no doubt that the weaver planned a very finely woven basket by the fineness of the bottom row. Perhaps the one who finished the basket could no longer see to weave so finely and added more split root to make it easier. Obtained by Mrs. L. C. Berg in 1935.

Previous owner: Lila Brougher Berg

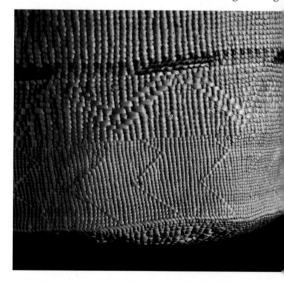

Detail of basket No. 702.

YEAR MADE: CA. 1920 YEAR OBTAINED: 1928

Doris Borhauer's Notes: This nice covered spruce root basket, with a rattle in the lid, was made about 1920 by a Sitka Thlingit Indian woman (name unknown). Purchased by Lila Brougher in 1928. This was one of the first baskets owned by her.

Previous owner: Lila Brougher Berg

YEAR OBTAINED: 1947

Doris Borhauer's Notes: This spruce root basket was made by a Sitka Thlingit Indian woman (date and weaver unknown). Purchased by Lila Berg in 1947 from the basket collection of Mrs. W. P. Mills.

Previous owner: Lila Brougher Berg

YEAR MADE: 1930   YEAR OBTAINED: 1947

Doris Borhauer's Notes: This large open spruce root basket was made by a Sitka Thlingit Indian woman (name unknown) in 1930. It was obtained from Mrs. W. P. Mills in 1947. This was one of the best and finest woven of her collection.

Previous owner: Mrs. W. P. Mills

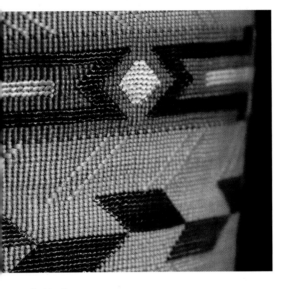

Detail of basket No. 715

YEAR MADE: 1932   YEAR OBTAINED: 1932

Doris Borhauer's Notes: This spruce root basket, with a braided handle (one side off), was made by a Thlingit Indian woman (name unknown) at Sitka in 1932. Purchased by Lila Brougher, U.S. government nurse, in 1932.

Previous owner: Lila Brougher Berg

YEAR MADE: CA. 1920   YEAR OBTAINED: 1955

Doris Borhauer's Notes: This unusual spruce root basket, woven in the shape of an iron kettle with legs, was made in Sitka about 1920 by a Sitka Thlingit Indian woman (name unknown). In 1955 it was obtained from Mrs. W. W. (Marie) Knight by Lila Berg.

Previous owner: Mrs. W. W. Knight, Lila Berg

YEAR MADE: 1800s?   YEAR OBTAINED: 1966

Doris Borhauer's Notes: This very large spruce root water tight basket was made in Sitka, Alaska, by a Thlingit Indian woman. The dark brown color indicates use and age. It was purchased in a spruce root basket collection in Sitka by Mr. Keller in 1906. The collection was taken to Skagway and placed in Mr. Keller's gift shop. This collection of baskets is thought to be one owned by Mr. Alexander M. Archangelski, a resident of Sitka in the early 1900's. This water basket was purchased at Keller's Gift Shop in Skagway, Alaska, May 1966.

Previous owner: perhaps Mr. Alexander M. Archangelski

❯❯ Baskets by Unknown Southeast Alaska Weavers

The following baskets are not identified with particular weavers and do not come from Sitka where the majority of baskets originated. However, they are still wonderful and interesting examples of basket weaving. Among the baskets is a copy of a Makah-style basket (No. 723, made by a Tlingit woman), an imitation of a China bowl, with a high degree of skill needed (No. 707) and the quintessential tourist basket (No. 727).

National Park Service Catalog No. 663

YEAR MADE: CA. 1925 YEAR OBTAINED: 1947

Doris Borhauer's Notes: This spruce root basket was made by a Wrangell Thlinget Indian woman about 1925. Name of weaver unknown. Purchased from the Wrangell curio store 1947 by Mrs. L. C. Berg. The black of the design represents wild geese flying and is made of the stem of maidenhair fern. The center of the pattern is grass dyed with native dye and is waves of the sea.

Previous Owner: Lila Brougher Berg

National Park Service Catalog No. 666

YEAR OBTAINED: 1961

Doris Borhauer's Notes: This small flat bowl was made by a Thlingit Indian of either Hoonah or Angoon and may be spruce root. Its imperfection may indicate the weaver was a child or a beginner. Its dark roots indicate its age. It was found in Sitka by Lila Berg in 1961.

Previous Owner: Lila Brougher Berg

Detail of basket No.707

National Park Service Catalog No. 707

YEAR MADE: CA. 1860 YEAR OBTAINED: 1946

Doris Borhauer's Notes: This unusual bowl-shaped spruce root basket was made by a Thlingit Indian woman of Yakutat about 1860. Miss Mae Mill's father, a merchant trader took it in trade from a Yakutat Indian. It was added to her collection. It is a salmonberry bowl. The designs on the inside as well as the outside make this a unique sample of Thlingit artistry. In 1946 this basket was obtained from Miss Mae Mills by Mrs. L. C. Berg. Design: the Butterfly-Klaythl-thlu Blanket border pattern, used before the purchase of Alaska from Russia.

Previous Owner: Miss Mae Mills, Lila Berg

National Park Service Catalog No. 713

YEAR MADE: CA. 1860 YEAR OBTAINED: 1962

Doris Borhauer's Notes: This old spruce root basket, with the unusual design, was made in Southeast Alaska by a Thlingit Indian over one hundred years ago. It was purchased from the Sportsman Curio Shop in Ketchikan in 1962.

Note for basket No. 713: This is the oldest documented basket in the collection, and is different from the other of the oldest baskets because it is decorated, most likely with maidenhair fern. The design itself is unusual, not one of the more common native geometric designs. One weaver thought the design was probably taken from Blue Willow China, which sometimes has a similar oriental design.

National Park Service Catalog No. 722

YEAR MADE: 1929

Doris Borhauer's Notes: This covered spruce root basket was made at Haines, Alaska, in 1929 by a Thlingit Indian woman (name unknown). The orange-colored grass in the design is reputed to be native dye, though the source is unknown. It was first owned by Miss Ruth

Green, a teacher at S.J.S. in 1928–30. Then owned by Lila Brougher, also a teacher at S.J.S.

Previous Owner: Miss Ruth Green, Lila Berg

National Park Service Catalog No. 723

YEAR OBTAINED: 1948

Doris Borhauer's Notes: This covered basket resembles those made of spruce roots by Thlingit Indians of Southeast Alaska, though it does not have the smooth finish of spruce roots. The grass pattern is entirely on the outside, just as the Thlingit weave their patterns so it may have been copied. The design resembles that of "worm tread" of Thlingit origin. Maker, date, origin unknown. Purchased in Sitka, Alaska in 1948.

Note: Although the notes from Doris Borhauer say that this basket "does not have the smooth finish of spruce roots," on examination it is made of spruce roots. It is likely that it was made in Sitka, although it cannot be confirmed.

The basket is somewhat unusual because the lid is flat, and typically rattle-top lids were not so flat. Also, the basket colors are faded on the outside. You can see in the photo on the right that inside there is a bright blue band, which shows on the outside as being dark gray.

National Park Service Catalog No. 725

YEAR MADE: CA. 1920 YEAR OBTAINED: 1929

Doris Borhauer's Notes: This small covered spruce root basket was made by a Thlingit Indian woman at Angoon, Alaska, about 1920. Name of weaver unknown. Obtained by Lila Brougher, teacher at S.J.S., March 1929.

Previous Owner: Lila Brougher Berg

National Park Service Catalog No. 727

YEAR MADE: 1932 YEAR OBTAINED: 1932

Doris Borhauer's Notes: This unusual covered spruce root basket was made at Angoon, Alaska, in 1932 by a Thlingit Indian woman (name unknown). The "ALASKA BASKET" is woven in maidenhair fern stems. The red arrow of the main pattern is colored with a concentrated uric acid; the white is the natural grass color and the bit of yellow from a weak hemlock bark solution. The black roots under the pattern are spruce roots dyed with blueberry juice. The rattle in the lid—stones from a grouse's crop. Purchased by 1932 by nurse L. Brougher.

Previous Owner: Lila Brougher Berg

DETAIL ON NEXT PAGE.

Detail of basket No. 727

YEAR OBTAINED: 1967

Doris Borhauer's Notes: This partially made spruce root basket was purchased at Keller's Gift Shop in Skagway, Alaska, May 1967.

YEAR MADE: EARLY 1900s
YEAR OBTAINED: 1969

Doris Borhauer's Notes: This spruce root basket with rattle in lid was owned by Mrs. Agnes Perez of Ketchikan, Alaska. She was born in 1892. This basket was given to Mrs. Perez when she was seventeen years old by a Thlingit woman from Kake, Alaska. The design is of grass- natural dyes. This basket is at least sixty years old. Purchased from Mrs. Perez May 29, 1969. Rattle in lid—"something inside basket"—*Too-duh-kuhk* Design: half-head of salmon berry—*Kunk-shu-yuk-kun-yuh-ty*. Spirit around the Head-Shaman's Hat pattern—*Shuh-dah-yay-ghee*. One of the oldest patterns, adaptable to all forms and sizes of baskets. Represents the mountain range as it descends to the water.

Previous Owner: Mrs. Agnes Perez

YEAR MADE: CA. 1880 YEAR OBTAINED: 1949

Doris Borhauer's Notes: This old and unusual covered spruce root basket was made in Southeast Alaska by a Thlingit Indian woman (name unknown) about 1880. It was from the basket collection of Mrs. W. P. Mills and was purchased from her by Lila Berg in 1949.

Previous Owner: Mrs. W. P. Mills, Lila Berg

YEAR MADE: 1800s   YEAR OBTAINED: 1963

Doris Borhauer's Notes: This old spruce root basket was purchased at a rummage sale in Portland, Oregon, in 1963. The weaver, time, place, materials are unknown, but we estimate, because of the color of the roots, that it is over one hundred years old. The lid, having a different design, could have belonged to another basket. There is evidence of a woven handle on the basket. Native dyes were used in the pattern.

YEAR OBTAINED: 1947

Doris Borhauer's Notes: This lovely covered spruce root basket was made by a Thlingit Indian woman of Southeast Alaska. Note the unusual design of salmon-berries on the cover top. Purchased at Pruell's Jewelry Store in Ketchikan by Mrs. L. C. Berg in 1947.

Previous Owner: Lila Brougher Berg

⊡ Index of Baskets by Catalog Numbers

About the Author

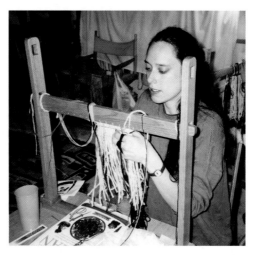

Photo taken by Clarissa Hudson.

Helen Dianne Dangel is Tlingit, from the Eagle Moiety, the Kaagwaantaan Clan, and the Wolf House. Helen works for the Sitka Tribe of Alaska as the Cultural Research Specialist. It is through her work with tribal elders and other informants that she is able to write this book. Helen was born in Juneau, Alaska, and currently resides in Sitka, Alaska, where she has many family ties. She and her husband have two children. Helen is a weaver, and has woven spruce root baskets, Ravenstail and Chilkat woolen pieces.